taste of the earth

CREATING NEW ZEALAND'S FINE WINE

taste of the earth

CREATING NEW ZEALAND'S FINE WINE

KEITH STEWART · PHOTOGRAPHS BY KEVIN JUDD

CRAIG
POTTON
PUBLISHING

TEXT: KEITH STEWART.
PHOTOGRAPHS: KEVIN JUDD.
DESIGN: ROBBIE BURTON.
EDITING: JANE PARKIN.
MAP: MAGGIE ATKINSON.
PRINTED BY PRINTLINK, WELLINGTON, NZ.

FIRST PUBLISHED IN 2001 BY
CRAIG POTTON PUBLISHING LTD,
98 VICKERMAN STREET,
PO BOX 555, NELSON, NEW ZEALAND.
www.craigpotton.co.nz

ISBN 0-908802-74-9

CONTENTS

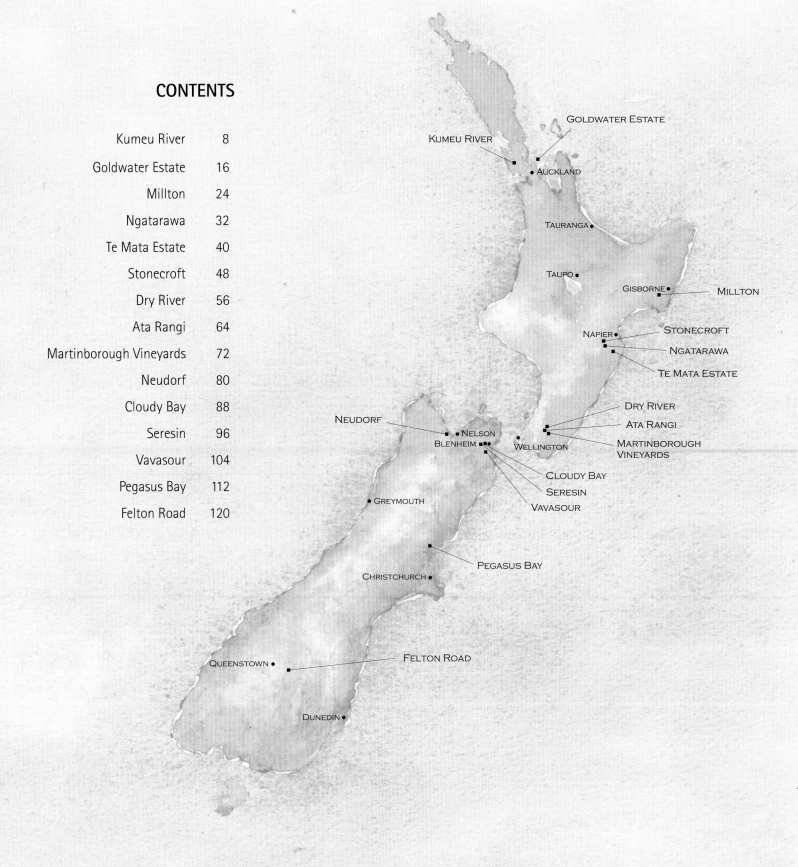

GOLDWATER ESTATE

KUMEU RIVER

AUCKLAND

TAURANGA

TAUPO

GISBORNE · — MILLTON

NAPIER · — STONECROFT

NGATARAWA

TE MATA ESTATE

DRY RIVER

ATA RANGI

NEUDORF

NELSON

BLENHEIM

WELLINGTON

MARTINBOROUGH VINEYARDS

CLOUDY BAY

SERESIN

VAVASOUR

GREYMOUTH

PEGASUS BAY

CHRISTCHURCH

FELTON ROAD

QUEENSTOWN

DUNEDIN

INTRODUCTION

Much is made of wines' origins, the plot of land on which it is grown and which, according to popular legend, invests every wine with an inimitable character of place that is discernible to the connoisseur, and bankable to the marketer. It is the Champagne in champagne, the Oporto in port and the Margaux in Chateau Margaux. But these are all old-world winegrowing regions where the boundary between physical and social geography is blurred in the bottle. What of the new world? Is there a definitive Marlborough in Cloudy Bay?

The answer can only ever be a tentative yes, because so many of the factors that contribute to any wine's character are imposed on the place where it is grown, and that process has only just begun in the new world. Foremost of these factors is grape variety, which is the single greatest influence on wine character. What quirk of history was it that took cabernet sauvignon to Bordeaux, or chardonnay to Chablis, and how could wines from either of these areas be considered outside of those varieties and the events that took them there? What if the Rheingau had been planted with chardonnay, not riesling?

As sauvignon blanc has become synonymous with Marlborough to international wine drinkers, the story of its arrival in the region is a good example of the arbitrary evolution of wine character in any place. It began with a young New Zealand winemaker, Ross Spence, who was inspired by the character of Sauvignon Blanc wines grown in California and on his return secured cuttings of the variety and planted them on his own West Auckland vineyard. A few years later, he took a bottle of his first Sauvignon Blanc to dinner with a couple of wine-industry friends who were impressed by its character. One of them, Montana's Peter Hubscher, determined it would be a suitable candidate for his company's new project in Marlborough. So it proved to be, and Marlborough's defining variety was planted on evidence of its performance in a West Auckland vineyard.

There were a number of other factors in favour of Marlborough suiting sauvignon blanc. In the first instance, the clones of the variety that were available were good quality, and not restrained by any viral problems or other disease. Further, sauvignon blanc was not only suited to Marlborough's climate and soils; it was an ideal variety for the industrial harvesting and processing Montana used in its vineyards and its new, stainless-steel winery. Finally, the lively aroma and flavour of sauvignon blanc was simple and forthright – exactly the style to appeal to new wine drinkers such as those in New Zealand, and especially in the United Kingdom.

Four lucky breaks for Sauvignon Blanc and Marlborough, each of which highlights the development of a place into a winegrowing region through the interaction of geography and people who are growing, making, selling and drinking wine. This book is a brief record of that process. It looks at 15 New Zealand winemakers and the evolution of their particular wine culture in their discrete locations.

All were intent on making the best wine possible, and all have owned and managed a particular vineyard from which they have drawn their grapes. In every sense these are the stories of a new wine culture, one which is different from any other but which, in its dependence on the land and its capricious nature, is remarkably similar to all wine cultures, everywhere.

KUMEU RIVER

KUMEU VALLEY, AUCKLAND

The Kumeu River story encapsulates the wine revolution in New Zealand: not just the discovery of terroir and the subsequent development of a winegrowing culture from which premium-quality wine can be produced, but also the rapid assimilation of a sophisticated national wine palate which is sensitive to international wine standards. In both, the Brajkovich family has been an influential catalyst since they bought their Kumeu Valley property in 1944.

The 5.25 hectare farm on the outskirts of Kumeu village was typical of the farms developed by Dalmatian immigrant families from the proceeds of labouring in their new country. From this small block divided by the main road the family produced cream from a small dairy herd, pigs, apples and peaches, pumpkins and strawberries, as well as table grapes and wine from the ubiquitous Albany Surprise.

It was wine which offered the most promise, and Mate Brajkovich was as innovative as any in developing the family prospects in this area. A larger vineyard was developed, exclusively using winemaking varieties including palomino, pinotage, and hybrids such as Siebel 5455 and Baco 22A, and by the mid fifties Mate was making a rough, dry red table

wine for home. Through its appearance at various Auckland parties frequented by Mate, this wine became one of the earliest markers of New Zealand's changing tastes under the influence of immigrant European cultures and the experience of soldiers recently returned from the war in Europe. Among the fans of Kumeu Dry Red were a group of artists shaping a new culture which was different from that of the truncated colony they had inherited – figures like A.R.D. Fairburn, Dick Scott and Colin McCahon

FAR LEFT: Lyre-trained chardonnay, Mate's vineyard.

OWNERS: THE BRAJKOVICH FAMILY

WINEMAKER: MICHAEL BRAJKOVICH

PRODUCTION: 25,000 CASES

TWENTY-SIX HECTARES OF ESTATE VINEYARDS, 47% CHARDONNAY, 31% MERLOT, 12% PINOT NOIR, 6% MALBEC AND 4% PINOT GRIS. SOME GRAPES ARE TAKEN FROM CONTRACT GROWERS IN THE KUMEU DISTRICT.

THE LEADING WINE HAS BEEN CHARDONNAY, FIRST WITH THE GROUND-BREAKING KUMEU CHARDONNAY, AND THEN MATE'S VINEYARD CHARDONNAY. MERLOT HAS LONG BEEN THE MAINSTAY OF REDS, AND RECENTLY THIS HAS BEEN ADVANCED BY ADDITIONS OF MALBEC AND THE DEVELOPMENT OF PINOT NOIR.

A budding dynasty: Marijana, Melba, Mate, Michael and Milan Brajkovich. (Photo: Marti Friedlander)

for whom table wine was a symbol of what was possible.

Mate Brajkovich worked assiduously at his vineyard (the cows and pigs were soon replaced by vineyard and winery), producing an eclectic range of labels and styles which included various sherries, ports, liqueurs and table wines all sold under the name San Marino. The fashionable new grape variety of the sixties, müller thurgau, was planted in the vineyard, and sales of wine at the farm gate were no longer enough to meet San Marino's marketing needs. Mate undertook weekly deliveries around Auckland in a Chevrolet van to service and expand his customer base.

With the white table wine boom of the late sixties and seventies, another 16 hectares was bought adjacent to the Kumeu property, and grapes were bought in from growers in Gisborne and Hawke's Bay to meet the burgeoning demand for wine. Yet, unlike a number of other West Auckland winemakers, San Marino remained a family company defined by the parameters of its home vineyards. As the domestic wine business flourished and the market became larger and more complex, and others expanded well beyond their West Auckland origins, planting vineyards in Gisborne, Hawke's Bay and Marlborough and expanding their humble operations into corporate ventures, the Brajkovich family was faced with some momentous decisions if they wanted to keep pace with the changes facing the industry.

At the time, Mate and Melba Brajkovich's eldest son Michael was studying oenology at the preferred training institute of Australian and New Zealand winemakers, Roseworthy College, and he was fully involved in the discussions on what the family should do. They decided to stay small and base themselves on their Kumeu property – a plan which demanded they make wine of the highest possible quality to meet the growing expectations of local consumers and the potential of export.

In Michael they believed they had the skill to make the wine; what they needed was the raw material for him to work with. The first major step was to redevelop their vineyards, replanting with new varieties which had the potential to produce wine of significantly higher quality than their current standard. In 1982 the palomino and hybrids were replaced by cabernet sauvignon and chardonnay; sauvignon blanc, cabernet franc and some more chardonnay followed in 1983. The family also had the opportunity early in 1983 to buy established merlot vineyards from Corbans, who were following the trend and developing vineyards in Marlborough. They bought an 8 hectare parcel, which is now the Kumeu River Waitakere Road vineyard, and in 1983 Michael made the family's first gold medal red wine from its merlot fruit.

It was their second stroke of luck. The first was the decision to plant chardonnay. When they decided to stay with their own land in Kumeu, Michael researched the possible varieties they would plant according to the prevailing conditions of humid, maritime climate and clay-rich soils. Although there was limited availability in 1982, and many of the clones available were virused or of limited value for premium-quality wine, the decision to try the Bordeaux classics cabernet sauvignon and franc, along with the already-established merlot, was influenced by the relative success of cabernet reds grown in the Kumeu Huapai district during the 1970s.

Family in charge: Michael, Paul, Melba and Milan.

Michael's research also showed that both chardonnay and sauvignon blanc had potential; but of the five from that initial redevelopment, only chardonnay and merlot have proven to be well suited. After 20 years of evaluation, there is no place for varieties which do not meet standards of quality and consistency. Both the cabernets have too often shown 'weedy' characters, and have been replaced by newer clones of merlot, which has become the mainstay of red wine production, with a supporting role for malbec, which contributes colour and tannin.

Sauvignon blanc has also been replaced by chardonnay, not because the wines were less than expected but simply because the savoury, richly flavoured Kumeu River wines were too much at odds with the fruit-burst styles of Marlborough to gain ready acceptance from wine drinkers. Kumeu River Chardonnay, by comparison, was such a success that more was needed, and sauvignon blanc has been replaced with new clones of chardonnay.

Varietal experimentation continues, however, with more short-term success than was the case earlier. Two new pinots – pinot noir and pinot gris – have been introduced, and both have attracted considerable interest and critical acclaim.

'We have always been interested in pinot noir, as it is a natural partner for chardonnay, which we know we can do well. When we first tried it with fruit from a grower, it was from the wrong clones. Now we have a vineyard that is 100% new Dijon clones, and it is looking good,' comments Michael Brajkovich.

11

Other, less obvious developments are also part of the replanting programme, with less vigorous rootstocks replacing the SO4 and 1202 which were standard in New Zealand back in the eighties. Now the selection includes riparia gloire, 101-14 and 420 A, all of which counter the fertile Kumeu soils, but the format of the vineyards is essentially the same as was established in 1982, with the vines trained to open the canopies using the lyre system. This increases airflow and sunlight penetration, and assists ripening, with two fruiting canes laid down each season.

Other aspects of vineyard management are direct responses to the demands of Kumeu's climate, which is humid and subject to sudden heavy rainfall. To moderate the effects of the rainfall on vineyard slopes, all are grassed down fully to facilitate run-off. But it is humidity and bird damage which have been the principal challenges to Michael's brother Milan, who is responsible for the vineyards.

Humidity provides perfect conditions for the development of botrytis and powdery mildew which can severely damage crops by reducing grape quality and undermining vine health. Milan's approach is a labour-intensive programme of persistent management of the vineyard environment to reduce the potential for fungal growth. Sprays are used, mostly copper and sulphur, with a minimal amount of fungicide, and all pruned cuttings are removed from the vineyards and burned to reduce the ambient spore count. Canopy management, however, makes the greatest contribution.

'The biggest factor in reducing bot strike is leaf plucking which increases air flow, reduces vineyard humidity and simply doesn't let conditions develop where botrytis can thrive,' Milan explains.

The results, if you know what to look for, can be found in Kumeu River's Chardonnays, which are invariably as clean as those from regions where humidity is not an issue.

The other pressing vineyard problem, bird strike, has effectively been solved by netting. In West Auckland, with its diversity of crops and orchards and large areas of nearby bush, birds have always been a particular problem. But the advantage of netting is not just that it prevents crop losses, which can be substantial; it also protects against the introduction of off characters from bird-damaged fruit and enables picking to occur when the fruit is ripe, not to beat the birds.

RIGHT: A sea of vines, Waitakere Road vineyard.

12

This is a thoroughly modern approach, but one that at a fundamental level does not seem too different from the viticulture practised in Europe's famous winegrowing regions for generations. Careful attention to detail is essential; it puts people in the vineyards on a daily basis throughout the year, either pruning, leaf plucking or picking (which is all done by hand), or simply keeping in touch and watching for signs that the vineyard has something to say.

'It is a culture of waiting for things to happen, of every year learning something different and modifying things slightly in the vineyard and in the winery. It is progress by learning what it is we can really do here,' says Michael Brajkovich.

There is also the matter of his own direction of the winemaking. It has had a profound influence not only on the quality and character of Kumeu River's wines but also on the way the rest of New Zealand's winemakers now approach chardonnay. Fundamentally, the process is similar to the 'watch, wait and carefully adjust' philosophy that drives the viticulture, and it is true that the same attention to detail and respect for the natural continuum of winegrowing and production permeate all levels of Kumeu River management. Yet the changes that Michael wrought from the beginning of his tenure were dramatic, simply by being aimed at the highest possible quality.

Initially there was the sudden appearance of expensive French oak in the winery, immediately influencing the taste and texture of Kumeu River wines, particularly the first Chardonnays which were emphatically different from anything most New Zealand wine drinkers had experienced. A visit to the winery 20 years later shows that this influence continues, although it has been refined by experience. Premium French oak remains a crucial ingredient in the wine, from barrel fermentation to the use of old oak for maturing Pinot Gris.

There were two other features of the Kumeu style which set it apart from the rest of the country at an early stage, and which Michael managed with rare skill, as either of them could have been too extreme to be acceptable. From 1982 he had been playing

'It is a culture of waiting for things to happen...'

around with malo-lactic fermentation, convinced that the style would be well suited to both chardonnay and sauvignon blanc, and that the reduction in the natural high acidity of Kumeu grapes and increased complexity would help both varieties. He was right, spectacularly so with the 1985 Kumeu River Chardonnay which was revolutionary in Australia and New Zealand. Malo-lactic fermentation has since become a feature of most premium Chardonnays in both countries, as well as continuing to be so at Kumeu River.

The other feature developed in France, where in 1983 Michael worked the vintage at Chateau Magdelaine in St Emilion. He was impressed by the use of wild yeast fermentations, as well as the general attitude of winemaking by husbandry rather than interference, and was inspired to use wild ferments in his 1984 red wines. In 1986, the second year of barrel fermentation of chardonnay and sauvignon blanc, his brother Milan and his assistant winemaker Nigel Tibbets argued that he should use the technique in these as well. It worked perfectly, and has become standard practice in all the Kumeu River wines, imparting a particular complexity to Kumeu and Mate's Vineyard Chardonnays that has become a defining characteristic. Other developments, such as whole-bunch pressing for chardonnay, lees management in barrel, and the development of delicate techniques suited to making Pinot Noir, are part of the continuous fine tuning at Kumeu River.

The success of the 20 year revolution from artisan producer to fine winecraft at Kumeu River can be measured by a comparison between the Chev van from which Mate used to sell his wine and the appearance of Melba Brajkovich and her sons at any one of the world's great wine fairs, usually as guests of honour. Kumeu River is now an international name, with marketing as sophisticated as its viticulture and winemaking.

The change is breathtaking, yet at its heart Kumeu River remains what it has always been, a family business. Under the direction of Melba since Mate died in 1992, all three brothers are now actively involved: Michael, Milan, and their youngest brother Paul who is responsible for marketing. The convivial hospitality Mate established remains, as do the vision and vitality which have turned the company into one of New Zealand's winemaking elite. And the revolution continues, with a new batch of wines from merlot, pinot noir and pinot gris emerging as worthy partners to those outstanding Kumeu and Mate's Vineyard Chardonnays.

'...of every year learning something different.'

GOLDWATER ESTATE

WAIHEKE ISLAND, HAURAKI GULF

There are few vineyards anywhere in the world as sublime as that of Goldwater Estate on Waiheke Island. Wedged into a comfortable tumble of hills gathered beside the blue Hauraki Gulf, the vines run their easy lines from pohutukawa tree to coast, lapping around the century-old bay villa that once served as a farmhouse when the land ran cattle. Yet behind this calm idyll lies a sharp business which delivers 30,000 cases of high-priced wine to customers across the globe, from Sydney to London and New York.

Goldwater Estate did begin as a dream, but like so many dreams the reality was tougher than either Kim or Jeanette Goldwater imagined. As yachties they frequently sailed past Waiheke and noted its gentle demeanour and its dry summers: here, they thought, was a place where grapes would grow much as they did in the Mediterranean where the Goldwater family had spent time living in Madrid. And a place where they might create a home which could capture some of the conviviality, the natural ambience of food and wine they had experienced with the Madriliños.

The decision to buy the Waiheke property was founded in that Spanish experience, and in the notion that in New Zealand they had the ability to create what they wanted – a feeling they could do anything provided they planned it properly. They were also looking for a place where they could spend the rest of their lives in comfort, a balmy place where they could get their fingers into the soil and live as part of a small community.

Waiheke offered all of these, and the chance to make something red in memory of the tender Valdepeñas which charmed the Goldwaters' Spanish Sundays, but Kim's research suggested something altogether more serious – cabernet sauvignon and its red cousins cabernet franc and merlot. In France these varieties are responsible for the most illustrious wines of Bordeaux, so the dream quickly turned to the possibility of excellence, even greatness.

OWNERS: JEANETTE AND KIM GOLDWATER
PRODUCTION: 30,000-PLUS CASES

THIS 12.5 HECTARE VINEYARD ON WAIHEKE ALSO TAKES GRAPES FROM 41 HECTARES IN MARLBOROUGH AND 8.3 HECTARES IN THE GIMBLETT ROAD DISTRICT OF HAWKE'S BAY.
FLAGSHIP WINES ARE CABERNET SAUVIGNON/MERLOT/CABERNET FRANC AND ESSLIN MERLOT. IT ALSO PRODUCES A WAIHEKE AND A MARLBOROUGH CHARDONNAY, AND MARLBOROUGH SAUVIGNON BLANC.

LEFT: Cabernet sauvignon above Putiki Bay, Waiheke Island.

17

Indeed, Kim Goldwater's ideal was none other than Chateau Margaux.

The vineyard was planted 50% in cabernet sauvignon, 40% in merlot and 10% in cabernet franc, all grafted onto the phylloxera-resistant rootstock, 1202. It was an exciting beginning for the Goldwaters, making the dream concrete, but the degree to which such a venture was exotic in the prevailing Waiheke Island culture came when the local council inadvertently sprayed the vineyard with the herbicide 245T. Its response was that the vineyard shouldn't have been there, as farming was exclusively agricultural, not horticultural.

'I think I would have accepted an apology and a promise not to do it again. But when they wouldn't speak to us except through lawyers it was our first wake-up call, the first sign that we were doing something very alternative,' Kim Goldwater remembers.

With that setback, the first full vintage was not until 1982, and it produced fruit every bit as good as expected.

'I knew from the very small crop from what was left in 1981 that we were going to make good wine. The grapes were fantastic, like nothing I had ever tasted before,' Goldwater says.

But it was not the grapes so much as the manner of harvesting which emphasised the philosophy behind Goldwater Estate. Pickers were a collection of neighbours, family and friends from around the Auckland area who came for a day in the vines and the experience of Jeanette's table, laden as it was with abundant flavours of sunshine and innovation. For many Aucklanders, Goldwater vintages were their introduction to the generous spirit of Mediterranean cuisine that had inspired their hosts, and it became one of the key ingredients in the romance of Waiheke which has made the island and its wines so popular.

Kim and Jeanette Goldwater, a shared enthusiasm.

But the Goldwaters were set for more serious destinations with their wines, especially in reaction to the quality of that first vintage. Their attention to the detail of quality saw them as very early followers of Richard Smart, whose canopy management ideas found form in their trellis systems and their ability to maintain that initial quality. Young cabernet sauvignon is notoriously precocious, looking fantastic in its first vintage but suffering a collapse in quality in subsequent years. Goldwater managed to avoid that, as much through good management as through the advantages of the vineyard site. Ever since, the aim of vine management at Goldwater Estate has been to get the canopy into balance.

On the clay soils of Waiheke, irrigation is not an issue. Dry farming has been the status quo since the vineyard was planted, although drought stress is an issue in abnormally dry years like 1983/ 84. Experience suggests to Kim Goldwater that the best results are from vines planted close and kept small, with low heads, and pruned to single vertical shoot positions. Rootstocks are now all low vigour – riparia gloire and 3309, rather than the 1202 originally used – and the vineyard is no longer cultivated as it once was, but is grassed down to help retain heat.

As with most vineyards of this age, most has been replanted in response to newly available, improved clones of all the principal varieties, and to allow expression of the lessons learned over the years. The last 2 acres of original cabernet sauvignon produced just 350 kilograms of fruit in its final harvest, but the quality was exceptional, and Goldwater believes that with time, and vine age, the whole vineyard will manage similar quality in more economic quantities.

In the winery, Goldwater has been very much in charge, learning from vintage to vintage by experience and through contact with a number of mentor winemakers who have freely shared their advice. In an age when high-tech presses are standard in most high-profile, new-world wineries, the Goldwaters' horizontal, moving-plate Vaslin is almost old fashioned. But this is very much in keeping with a winemaking philosophy which could be deemed a traditional new-world approach, moderated by old-world standards.

The key is to respond to results, and if the standards being achieved are good, then there is no need to change. The press works well, so there is no need to change, and the

'I couldn't think of anything I would want to do more.'

winery techniques, such as yeast inoculation, warm fermentations and pumping-over in closed tanks, can be seen in any new-world winery. One change has been the move to 225 litre French barrels, rather than the original puncheons, and more meticulous barrel-ageing programmes in keeping with the variety and character of the wines they hold. A mix of science and craft, driven by the results in the vineyard.

'I have become more confident in knowing how to achieve, and to let the wine make itself as much as possible. I have found that it is better to know what you have, rather than try for something you might get,' Goldwater says.

One surprise in light of the Chateau Margaux-inspired beginning, is that the estate's top-priced wine is now a pure merlot, known as Esslin, which sells out rapidly in New York but is beyond the ken of most local wine buffs. Perhaps this is a sign of how much Goldwater Estate has become a cosmopolitan entity, with the United States now its biggest market.

Another sign is the quantity of wine now being sold – significantly more than can be produced from 12.5 hectares of Waiheke vineyards. It is this which signifies the substantive change in the Goldwaters' dream, for this is no longer a romance, it is business. Gone are the days when Kim and Jeanette alone managed the vineyard, winemaking and marketing, and when Jeanette found a likely employee sorting through the rubbish at the local tip.

'We are getting old, and a few years ago realised that we couldn't continue as we were. We were faced with the decision either to sell up and move on, or to stay and employ people to help us with the work. We figured we could get another 20 years in the industry if we could increase our workforce. The fact is, you can't do that on a few acres on Waiheke,' says Kim.

So they looked further afield, both for production and markets. The international exposure their impressive reds had gained for them showed there was an export market for their wine, and especially for New Zealand white wines. Unfortunately, theirs was a red-only vineyard, so they looked for alternative grape sources as well, and found that in

ABOVE: Merlot.

LEFT: 'I have found it is better to know what you have...'

21

ABOVE: A thriving little vineyard.

RIGHT: An idyll wedged between the sea and a new island suburbia.

Marlborough there were opportunities to expand through the availability of grapes and of Rapaura Vintners, contract winemakers who had been established to make wine for producers who did not have a Marlborough winery of their own.

So Goldwater Estate became a producer of Marlborough Sauvignon Blanc and Chardonnay, grown under contract and made under Kim Goldwater's direction at Rapaura Vintners. The little Waiheke vineyard has grown, with Marlborough now the source of the majority of the estate's production, most of which is exported to North America and Europe.

Not that Waiheke has suffered. On the contrary, the little vineyard is now thriving, a destination for wine tourists, complete with a new winery and a new chardonnay vineyard made up of clones 6, 15 and 95 tucked into the next tree-fringed bay. Kim and Jeanette Goldwater, now international wine figures, remain as keen as ever to get around the farmhouse table for conversation, good food and a few glasses of wine. Much better wine than Valdepeñas.

For Goldwater the issues of vineyard and winemaking have always been driven by cultural, rather than scientific, business or production rationales. The location was primarily chosen because it appealed as a place to live towards retirement, and wine was grown because it suited the lifestyle. The decision to pursue an ideal based on a wine as extreme in quality and reputation as Chateau Margaux was a natural consequence of the Goldwaters' aim to achieve the best possible outcomes, given the circumstances of their chosen spot. There was a significant element of luck in the capacity of a site chosen for its emotional appeal to grow grapes of a high enough standard for premium-quality red wine. In developing the skills to grow and make such wine, the primary influence has been an open attitude to learning from the best available evidence, and applying those lessons to a specific physical and social geography.

Finally, the decision to expand was also generated by a lifestyle choice, to stay at home and continue their chosen dream for as long as possible. It has made their social life more cosmopolitan and less private than they would have imagined it when they first bought the land, but as Jeanette Goldwater says, 'I couldn't dream of anything I would want to do more.'

MILLTON

MANUTUKE, GISBORNE

The hallmark of Millton Vineyard wines has always been their harmonious nature, but the path to this producer's ultimate success has been far from harmonious. James and Annie Millton's struggle to establish their winery has been compounded by their determination to manage their vineyards and winemaking according to the holistic, 'organic' approach promoted by the German philosopher Rudolf Steiner. Not only was this an unfashionable idea when they first embraced it, but it also put them into direct conflict with the industrial farming attitudes of most of the wine industry, and in particular with the practices of Annie's father John Clark.

Compounding these problems was the geography of their land in Gisborne, which to viticulturists seemed the most unlikely place for an experiment in organic winegrowing. Gisborne's fertile soils and inclination towards high moisture levels throughout the growing season were factors in the region's reputation for being a haven for disease and pests, demanding the most extreme chemical control programmes in the country.

But James Millton was not easily deterred. He trained in winemaking at Mainz in Germany, and spent part of his early career working in wineries in Germany and in France, in Burgundy and the Loire Valley. He came to Gisborne because it was Annie's home; her family were already farming grapes for the local wine industry on a reasonably large scale.

Partly because of the climatic conditions, and partly because of its isolation, Gisborne, unlike most of New Zealand's winegrowing regions, never attracted the enthusiasts for high-quality wine who have led the transformation of the industry from industrial production of alcohol beverages to geographically individual winegrowing. With the exception of the Irwin family at Matawhero, Gisborne was, and remains, dominated by large wine corporations and their factory mentality, a culture which has nurtured the cash cropping of

LEFT: Naboth's vineyard, a rare hill site above the plain.

OWNERS: ANNIE AND JAMES MILLTON
WINEMAKER: JAMES MILLTON
PRODUCTION: 15,000 CASES

TWENTY-FIVE HECTARES OF VINEYARDS IN DIFFERENT SITES AROUND THE GISBORNE REGION, AT TE ARAI, RIVERPOINT, OPOU, AND THE NABOTH'S HILLSIDE VINEYARD AT MANUTUKE.

CHARDONNAY HAS BEEN THE MOST CONSISTENT, PREMIUM WINE, AND RIESLING HAS ALSO PERFORMED REGULARLY AND WELL. CHENIN BLANC WINES, EITHER DRY OR SWEET ACCORDING TO VINTAGE, ARE HIGHLY REGARDED AND IMPRESSIVE. RED WINES HAVE BEEN A LESSER PART OF THE RANGE.

'This is what we have, and we must work in harmony with it.'

grapes to the detriment of advances made in high-quality winegrowing.

In this environment it was always going be difficult for James Millton to apply the knowledge he had gained in the leading districts of Europe. This situation was made perfectly clear when he began work on the Clark family vineyards which were made up predominantly of bulk-producing varieties, Siebel 5455, pinotage, chasselas and müller thurgau. Millton saw the future in quality, not commodity, and encouraged Annie's parents to plant sauvignon blanc, semillon, riesling and the variety that had taken his attention in the Loire, chenin blanc.

The results were enough to impress a traditionalist like John Clark, but not enough to divert him from the commodity agriculture which was deeply rooted in his farming history, from sheep to grapes. And certainly not enough to allow Millton to begin experimenting with the ideas he had found in Rudolf Steiner's seminal book, *Agriculture*. Although the Millton Vineyard winery was built at Manutuke in 1984, and the first wines attracted critical and consumer interest around the country, James Millton was unhappy, and uncertain about the validity of his ideas, so in 1986 he took himself back to France for vintage and a chance to consider his situation in a more wine-friendly community.

In France he rediscovered the detailed husbandry of winegrowing, in particular its sensitivity to the land, and an inherent respect for a natural process of growing and winemaking. He returned enthusiastic and confident he could assert his organic ideals and make premium wine. 'After the French experience I knew I wasn't so nutty,' he recalls.

He secured part of the family vineyard for his trials, to which in 1986 he added the varieties cabernet sauvignon, merlot and chardonnay. He also began a development unheard of in Gisborne, where the norm is machine harvesting: he planted a vineyard on a steep hillside, which he called Naboth's Vineyard. In a fit of experimentation, Naboth's contained 13 different grape varieties, as it was the only way the Milltons could find out what it would grow best. It had become apparent that the key to their future was the land and what they could get it to produce for them.

'I make no claims that Gisborne is the chosen place for winegrowing. Nor do I have any aspirations to make it so. This is what we have, and we must work in harmony with it. I *will* say we have turned over more stones here than many winegrowers who have stony sites,' James Millton says.

He has also applied Steiner's biodynamics to viticulture with notable success, and now has a following for his 'Biogro'-labelled wines among organic supporters around the world. Not that the now-fashionable organics is ever considered a peg on which to hang Millton's marketing plan: in their opinion it is simply the best way to grow grapes and make wine.

'I'm a logical person, and inquisitive, and we have identified that biodynamics offers a map of the soul and how you can be a part of it, not apart from it. It is about the rhythm of life that modern agriculture, medicine and education is attempting to deny, but we think the evidence is there that this is the only way to get the best from the land. Our best wines are always those from the grapes which have had the minimum interference in the vineyard,' he says.

He also takes note of vineyard performance, and like any successful viticulturist has culled any varieties which fail to perform. Already Naboth is down to just two: pinot noir and chardonnay. Across the estate all cabernet sauvignon and cabernet franc is gone, hardly more than a decade after it was planted. Red wine responsibility (given Millton believes there should always be a red wine from the winery) rests with merlot, but in light of its unconvincing performance he is running a trial on malbec to see if it will fit the red wine bill more effectively.

'I am attracted to malbec because it makes *paysanne* wine. It is virile, uncomplicated, slightly roguish, and you just drink it,' he explains.

A fine sense of rural style – Annie and James Millton.

Riesling remains, partly for nostalgic reasons and partly because its grace suits the Millton style, although it is unlikely to become their leading variety. What has done well is chardonnay: there has been an expansion of its share of the vineyard, as well as experimentation with the white Rhone Valley variety, voignier. But it is chenin blanc which attracts most attention for the future for the winery. It is not a grape variety with a great track record in Gisborne, but Millton has never made easy choices, and there is a sense that its working-class history in New Zealand, as a commodity variety with the potential to turn from ugly duckling to soaring swan, is part of its appeal.

Without doubt it thrives under the Millton regime, and with Chenin Blanc there are

few producers outside France who have had the level of success that Millton has. And because, as James Millton continues to insist, it is a matter of viticulture before winemaking, and of what will do well in the vineyard, chenin blanc has virtually selected itself.

'Everything is an expression of site,' he says, and if you press him on the structure and mineral components of his soils he will defer to the worms.

'Count the worms,' he says, reaching for a spade. 'Dig one sod and count the worms. That will tell you whether the soil is healthy and in balance.'

There is scientific evidence to support his claim, and worms are part of the organic revolution which is stirring in high-profile vineyards all around the world, as the intensive viticultural practices of winegrowers are forcing people to consider the health of their fundamental natural systems.

As with the majority of the Gisborne winegrowing region, The Millton Vineyards' vineyard sites all have an abundance of alluvial, fine-textured soil delivered by frequent floods down the short, young rivers that dissect the plains. The soil profiles do not change substantially from site to site, which makes selection of phylloxera-resistant rootstock much easier than it could otherwise be. Many vineyards, including the older portions of Millton, were originally planted on their own roots, but the spread of phylloxera reached a crisis in 1986, and the only solution is grafting of all vines. Initially vines were grafted onto SO4 and 5BB, but the question of their vigour in the high-fertility soils and relatively high rainfall of Gisborne saw them soon replaced by 101-14 and 3309. These, too, are likely to be replaced in future planting by the hybrid rootstock variety Gravesac-Fercal because of its resistance to wood fungus.

Fungus, in the form of botrytis, is one of the pressing issues in Gisborne, because of the relatively high humidity and rainfall in the latter stages of the growing season. It is also one of the principal reasons why chenin blanc, a variety which produces superb botrytis-affected wines in Vouvray and other Loire Valley regions, is to the fore in James Millton's planning.

The reaction of industrial winegrowing to fungal control has traditionally been a heavy spray regime of broad-spectrum, synthetic fungicides aimed at killing any fungus that should appear in the vineyards. This system has effectively failed, as various fungal

ABOVE: Mechanical weeding a natural alternative to herbicide.

LEFT: Pruned and ready for spring – established vines at Manutuke.

diseases have become resistant to the sprays, while the organic approach at Millton is now seen as being especially effective for the long-term management of vineyards under risk.

The aim is to establish a vineyard environment which, through leaf plucking and other forms of canopy control, is not conducive to the development of fungus. Understanding the fungal cycle and its conditions is imperative; and based on the fact that spore growth is at its peak 24 hours before the full moon each month, applications of organic controls such as calcium, casurina or silica are applied. Exactly how, and what particular form is chosen, depends on the state of the crop. Silica dust, for example, will waterproof grape bunches, and there are other conditions better suited to spraying or ground applications.

There is a similar approach in the winery – everything in balance, with positives being nurtured rather than negatives being destroyed – but for all its natural harmony the defining feature remains human control. Crops are maintained at low levels to enhance intensity of flavour, richness and texture, and French oak barrels remain a feature of the winery, although their presence is less obvious in the wines than it is in many prestige labels. Fermentations are all encouraged but not induced, and indigenous yeasts are the normal way, with low malic acid levels determining a low proportion of malo-lactic fermentation.

There is at The Millton Vineyards an air of gentle certainty, a sense that the process is a way of life, not a scheme or a programme, and that the most intense activity going on is one of watching the vineyard and wines and waiting to see what they will do. If they deviate from what James Millton believes is the appropriate course, they will be encouraged not to stray. Insects, botrytis, wine infections will be controlled according to the limits of the closed system in which the wines are grown and made, always with an eye to balance beyond, as well as within, the wines themselves.

RIGHT: Manutuke vineyards in full summer flush.

NGATARAWA

HERETAUNGA PLAINS, HAWKE'S BAY

Ngatarawa's roots go way back to the turn of the twentieth century in Henderson, West Auckland, where Assid Abraham Corban, Alwyn Corban's great-grandfather, established a small 4 hectare vineyard. For three generations the Corban family made wine in Henderson, turning Corbans into one of the largest and most influential winemaking companies in the country until it was absorbed by Montana in 2000. By that time the Corban family were no longer involved, having sold their controlling interest to Rothmans in the late 1960s, but under Alwyn's father Alex Corban the company had instigated a series of developments in viticulture and winemaking which were the first steps in the modernisation and subsequent conversion of the wine industry to quality production.

It was the absence of the Corban family from this modern industry which prompted Alwyn to establish a new Corban winemaking regime. Alwyn had graduated from Auckland University with a degree in Mathematics, then took his sense of family tradition to Gisborne to work the 1973 vintage. He enjoyed the experience so much he decided to act on his intuition, and took himself off to Massey University for a further two years' study for a diploma in Biotechnology, and then to the University of California, Davis, for a Masters degree in Food Science (viticulture and enology).

'I wasn't forced into the wine industry by the family, not in a direct way, but I felt that I was losing my family heritage when Corbans was sold. When I tried the wine industry, I liked the feel of it, and so I went for it,' he explains.

His return from California took him to a job with McWilliams in Hawke's Bay in 1977, and with his eyes open for winegrowing prospects he spent a lot of time touring about the countryside evaluating

FAR LEFT: A re-invented landed gentry in the old thoroughbred stables.

OWNERS: BRIAN CORBAN AND ALWYN CORBAN

WINEMAKER: ALWYN CORBAN

PRODUCTION: 35,000 CASES

ESTATE-GROWN FRUIT PROVIDES 30% OF TOTAL PRODUCTION, WITH SOME SAUVIGNON BLANC FROM MARLBOROUGH FOR EXPORT, AND THE BALANCE COMING FROM GISBORNE AND HAWKE'S BAY GROWERS.

CURRENTLY THE ESTATE VINEYARDS COVER 11 HECTARES OF TAKAPAU SANDY LOAM SOILS SOUTH-WEST OF HASTINGS ON THE HERETAUNGA PLAINS; A FURTHER 12 HECTARES ARE YET TO BE PLANTED. THE SITE IS FLAT, AND THE SOILS A COMPLEX MIX OF LIGHT, SANDY, RED AND YELLOW/BROWN LOAMS THAT ARE VERY FRIABLE AND HAVE HIGH PHOSPHATE RETENTION AND GOOD INFILTRATION. BENEATH ARE STONES AND GRAVEL. THE CLIMATE IS DRY AND WARM, WITH MODERATE RISK FROM SPRING FROSTS.

THE VINEYARD IS PLANTED IN
CHARDONNAY, CABERNET SAUVIGNON,
MERLOT, SAUVIGNON BLANC AND RIESLING.
OF THESE, ALL HAVE PRODUCED HIGHLY
RATED WINES, WITH CHARDONNAY AND
CABERNET SAUVIGNON MERLOT UNDER THE
GLAZEBROOK AND ALWYN LABELS BEING
CONSISTENTLY RANKED AMONG THE REGION'S
BEST, AS HAVE THE BOTRYTIS-AFFECTED SWEET
RIESLINGS.

'...it is only from now on that we will
see the influence of Ngatarawa, the
place, on wine quality.'

potential vineyard sites among the sheep farms and orchards. As its own long history in
viticulture indicated, Hawke's Bay seemed to him to be perfectly suited to winegrowing,
and he was particularly interested in the Ngatarawa because of its suitable soils and dry,
warm climate, in spite of it having no history of viticulture at all. At the same time one of
the largest landowners in the Ngatarawa district, Gary Glazebrook, was also considering
the option of planting grapes for wine production.

Glazebrook's Washpool Station occupied swathes of Ngatarawa land, and both he
and Alwyn Corban were using Kim Salonius as a sounding board for their ideas and as a
source of answers to their questions. Salonius, a Canadian-born medievalist and proprietor of the tiny Eskdale wine estate, was a pioneer of classic winegrowing and table wine
production in Hawke's Bay at a time when the industry was founded on cheap fortified
wines. He was responsible for some of Hawke's Bay's first modern Chardonnay, Cabernet
Sauvignon and Gewürztraminer, and in his attitudes as much as his wines provided a
stimulus to those who saw a future for a different sort of wine industry in New Zealand.
Both Corban and Glazebrook, as well as Stonecroft's Alan Limmer, found inspiration in
Salonius's ideas, and through him they met and decided to pursue their goals together at
Ngatarawa.

In January 1981 they formed Ngatarawa Wines, a 50/50 partnership between the
Glazebrook family and Alwyn Corban, based at the Glazebrook family stables and private
racecourse on Ngatarawa Road, and with Alwyn Corban as winemaker. Later that year
they planted 8 hectares of vineyard adjacent to the old stables in the varieties
chardonnay, riesling, cabernet sauvignon, merlot, gewürztraminer, cabernet franc, malbec
and semillon. The following year a further 3.9 hectares of sauvignon blanc and a little
more riesling were added, all of which were planted on their own roots.

Initially the plan was to get the vineyard established and then to dry farm it without
irrigation, on the basis that the best European vineyards were similarly managed, and
natural water shortage appeared to be an advantage in winegrowing for high quality.
Unfortunately, the soils have such limited water-holding capacity that the dry growing
seasons put the vines into drought stress too early for the grapes to get fully ripe. There
was also a problem with full cultivation of the site, and the light topsoil was severely
eroded in windy conditions, so adjustments were quickly made to cope with these issues.

Drip irrigation has made for much more accurate management of water supply during the season, and grassing down the vineyards keeps the top layer of soil secure, as well as helping the overall soil structure. The one disadvantage has been the slightly lower vineyard temperatures with grass cover.

Another major issue arose with the widespread virus infection of the vines – a major problem throughout the wine industry at the time, and one which had a debilitating effect on production of premium-quality wines. Cabernet sauvignon was particularly badly affected, with leaf-roll virus undermining the ability of the vines to fully ripen their fruit and giving rise to problems of leafy/weedy characters, imbalanced acidity and light, short flavours in the wines. Similar problems existed in riesling, cabernet franc and merlot, although chardonnay appeared to be advantaged by its particular virus infection, especially in the Mendoza clone, with hen and chicken bunches producing small crops, and the proportion of small berries in the crop giving greater intensity and good fruit/acid/sugar balance.

There was also the problem of phylloxera, and the vineyard for most of its early life was in a constant state of being reconstituted with better clones, new virus-free material, and the introduction of phylloxera-resistant rootstocks. Initially the stocks used were all SO4, partly because of their availability and the limited knowledge of their potential in Ngatarawa soils. Since 1995 the preferred rootstocks have been low vigour 101-14 and 3309, both riparia-rupestris hybrids. The original 8 hectares is now completely gone, with the current estate of 23 hectares all on new, adjacent land.

Viticultural management has also been adapted to Scott-Henry trellis systems, leaf plucking, tucking and other intensive canopy management, as well as crop thinning at veraison to improve flavour intensity and balance. Attention is also paid to variations within maturity levels across the vineyard so as to narrow the band of maturity and use maturity variation as a winemaking option, introducing greater wine complexity and acting as a tool for better natural balance in the wines. The intention was to do as much of the winemaking as possible in the vineyard, but while there are certain fruit characteristics which come through in the wines, the link between vineyard and wine does not always emerge.

Perhaps this is because their systems remain young. To date the principal viticultural

Maintaining a heritage in wine, Alwyn Corban and his father Alex.

progress has been towards understanding the vineyard and its requirements, measuring the performance of likely varieties within the parameters of this site, and developing a suitable management system to control it. In Corban's opinion the site itself has had little chance to assert its character on the wines in anything other than a cursory fashion.

'Until now human intervention has had a major part to play. The quality factor has been what people have been doing, not the site itself, and it is only from now on that we will see the influence of Ngatarawa, the place, on wine quality,' he says.

Recently there has also been a change in the makeup of the company, with Alwyn's cousin, Henderson lawyer Brian Corban, taking over Gary Glazebrook's 50% share and making Ngatarawa a complete Corban family reconstruction. It is a change Alwyn is very happy about, removing the separation and conflicts between the winegrowing and winemaking functions of the previous relationship.

Since early on in the company's life, marketing had also posed serious problems. An imbalance in the mix of wine labels and qualities has put pressure on profitability, in part because of problems in the vineyard, but primarily because of the size of production and too much attention paid to wines at the top end which were in short supply but sold themselves on reputation alone. Certainly the effect of virus in the vineyards posed problems for wines at the bottom of the range, but as this was gradually resolved the company had the opportunity to redress the balance and vigorously push growth brands.

A critical event in this development came six years ago with the decision to abandon the concept of estate-only production and expand the grape source to independent growers. One result is that the winery is larger now than originally intended, helping profitability, and this in turn has permitted more attention on the details of quality at the top of the range, with an impressive new collection of black-labelled wines called 'Alwyn' recently introduced to fit into the highest-quality bracket.

'I am happy with it now. The scale of the operation means it is much easier to survive than it was,' says Corban.

Because of the degree of learning demanded by the virgin viticultural country of Ngatarawa, winemaking has changed substantially since the first vintages, none more so than Chardonnay. One of the keys to this has been the change from reductive winemaking – eliminating all possibilities of oxygen from the process and applying total control – to

LEFT: Chardonnay.

the current oxidative approach which seeks to manage the natural oxygen environment of wine fermentation to the benefit of both texture and complexity in the finished wines. Malo-lactic fermentation has also undergone an evolution from partial contributions, to total fermentation of all component wines, to its use now only in some wines but not in others. It is indicative of the change that the top wine, Alwyn Chardonnay, has no malo-lactic at all.

'It is a matter of looking at the sort of malo that we get here, and then adapting it. Palate texture has always been important to me, and a lot of this hangs around malo, so we are fine tuning it all the time,' says Corban.

Comparatively, Sauvignon Blanc is made much the same as it was initially, after a number of years of experimentation. Now its reductive processing and cool fermentation show how dependent this variety's international reputation is on pure, simple, unmodified fruit character.

One of the characteristics of Ngatarawa's growing environment is riesling's tendency to grow botrytis at late stages of ripeness and to nurture it under the normally dry conditions of late autumn, allowing for the development of high-quality sweet wines which have become a feature of the winery. However, the strength of Ngatarawa since its early days has been its premium-quality cabernet sauvignon-based red wines. This range now includes Merlot as well as Cabernet Sauvignon/Merlot blends, and the recent addition of Syrah, a variety which is proving to have great potential in the district.

Again, the winemaking is in a state of development, with experimentation continuing even as the top wines are being recognised for their high standards of winegrowing and winemaking. After 20 years, nothing has been confirmed other than a relaxation of attitude in the winery and more focus on every detail in the vineyard. Oak is important, and more detailed work is being done on refining structural factors such as tannins and pH in the vineyard, but it will not be until the vineyard's true character is fully understood that any degree of certainty will exist in the winery. Only then will a definitive Ngatarawa style begin to emerge.

RIGHT: The old stables at Ngatarawa.

TE MATA

HAVELOCK NORTH, HAWKE'S BAY

It may have had four different names, but Te Mata's 1892 vineyard is the oldest fine winegrowing site in New Zealand, first planted by the owner of Te Mata Station, Bernard Chambers, in 1892, and containing *'Pinots... and black Hamburghs'*, according to visiting viticulturist Romeo Bragato in 1895. The vineyard was originally called *Mamelon* in reference to the breast-shaped hill against which it lay. It was later called Swarthmoor in honour of the Chambers family's Quaker history, then became BDM (Buck, Dewar, Morris) when these three took over the property as part of the purchase of Te Mata Estate winery in 1974. Recently it has been renamed 1892 in honour of its longevity.

The estate is an unusual phenomenon in a young country with an even younger wine story, yet more remarkable is its performance over a century of winegrowing. Early on it contributed to the first known international awards for New Zealand red wine, at the Franco-British Exhibition in London in 1909, and 80 years later Elston Chardonnay was voted top white wine at the London International Wine Challenge. All this has been achieved with very little viticultural manipulation other than paying due care and atten- tion to the vines, and being prepared to accept the small crops they produce – as little as 4.5 tonnes per hectare during Bernard Chambers' time. Indeed, 1892 responds poorly to interference.

'Old BDM never had any irrigation, and its vines always looked a bit crook, with short shoots, that sort of thing,' says winemaker Peter Cowley. 'When we replanted part of

it recently we stuck in a bit of irrigation, but it was awful: the wine just didn't come anywhere near what we had come to expect from the vineyard. It just likes to be left alone to get on with growing grapes.'

Early in the 1970s it was exactly the sort of vineyard that friends John Buck and Michael Morris

FAR LEFT: The architecture at the Coleraine vineyard was a landmark before its wine was.

OWNERS: MICHAEL AND JUNE MORRIS, WENDY AND JOHN BUCK

WINEMAKER: PETER COWLEY

PRODUCTION: 35,000 CASES

THE WINERY AND 26 HECTARES OF VINEYARD ARE AT TE MATA ON THE OUTSKIRTS OF HAVELOCK NORTH; 32 HECTARES ARE AT NGATARAWA; AND A FURTHER 120 HECTARES AT WOODTHORPE ON THE SOUTHERN BANK OF THE TUTAEKURI RIVER.

SOILS VARY THROUGHOUT THE SITES, WITH TE MATA DISTRICT SOILS EITHER LIGHT VOLCANIC OVER SILICA PANS, OR LIMESTONE AND SANDSTONE ON THE STEEPER SLOPES, WITH OLDER GRAVEL AND SOIL ON 10,000- YEAR-OLD SEDIMENTARY DEPOSITS KNOWN LOCALLY AS RED METAL FURTHER AWAY FROM TE MATA PEAK'S FOOTHILLS. AT NGATARAWA ARE SHALLOW-PHASE NGATARAWA LOAMS, LIGHT SOILS OVER RED METAL; AND AT WOODTHORPE A MIX OF SHALLOW-PHASE TAKAPAU SOILS, LESS RED IN COLOUR, WITH 40CM OF LIGHT TOPSOIL OVER 30 METRES OF RED METAL.

THE CLIMATE IS WARM AND DRY
THROUGHOUT THE GROWING SEASON, WITH
SOME FROST RISK AT NGATARAWA, AND
SUMMER MAXIMUMS AROUND 35°C IN
SHELTERED LOCATIONS. BOTH NGATARAWA
AND HAVELOCK NORTH HAVE AN AVERAGE
DAILY MAXIMUM ABOVE 20°C THROUGH THE
PEAK RIPENING MONTHS OF JANUARY,
FEBRUARY AND MARCH, WITH WOODTHORPE
MARGINALLY COOLER.

THE LEADING WINE IN NEW ZEALAND HAS
BEEN COLERAINE, A BLEND OF CABERNET
SAUVIGNON, CABERNET FRANC AND MERLOT,
AND THE WINERY HAS AN IMAGE AS A
PRODUCER OF PRESTIGE RED WINE, WITH
AWATEA CABERNET/MERLOT AND BULLNOSE
SYRAH MAKING UP AN ACCLAIMED TRIO OF
LABELS. INTERNATIONALLY, HOWEVER, TE
MATA ESTATE IS KNOWN AS MUCH FOR
ELSTON CHARDONNAY, AND THIS WINE HAS
DEVELOPED A STRONG FOLLOWING IN
EUROPEAN FINE WINE CIRCLES.

had been looking for as a foundation for their winemaking plans. They had recognised in Tom McDonald's Cabernet Sauvignons Hawke's Bay's potential for growing high-quality red wines based on cabernet sauvignon, and in New Zealand's oldest winegrowing province they were looking for sites where they could do the same on their own behalf.

They found Te Mata, where they bought the winery and Chambers' original vineyard block, and Wendy and John Buck purchased 2 hectares of bare slope opposite, at the foot of Te Mata Peak. They called it Coleraine and built their house there. BDM then contained cabernet sauvignon and a collection of hybrids, with a small parcel of the Hungarian white variety, furmint. The hybrids and furmint were ripped out, but the cabernet sauvignon, after some tidying up, was used for wine.

With this and some cabernet sauvignon acquired from an old block that had once been part of Bernard Chambers' Terraces vineyard next door to BDM, and now known as Awatea, the newly formed Te Mata Estate set out to see if something smart could be made with the remnants of New Zealand's original fine wine industry.

'Our ideas were based on claret, on the classic red wines of Bordeaux. Not necessarily big wines, but aromatic and complex with the ability to age,' recalls John Buck.

Nothing if not a traditionalist, John Buck's focus has been firmly on Bordeaux ever since. In the form and disposition of the buildings and vineyards, in its commercial acumen and the style of its marketing, and in its sense of vinicultural propriety he has continued to fashion Te Mata in the manner of a Bordeaux estate. He has also measured Te Mata's winemaking standards against those of Bordeaux's most illustrious estates, so the trial wines the new Te Mata Estate made from BDM and Awatea fruit were subject to rigorous evaluation.

That the vineyards measured up is not disputed, for that 1980 Te Mata Cabernet Sauvignon, its companion 1981 version, and the first Coleraine and Awatea wines of the 1982 vintage are arguably the most influential New Zealand red wines made in the modern era. They won awards and critical acclaim, and grabbed the attention of other winemakers, in spite of a lack of sophistication in the winery. The key was obviously the vineyard.

'What those wines did for us was prove the potential of our vineyards. They gave us a feeling of optimism. We were certain we had something special in our sites, and

Coleraine and 1892 are still our two best vineyards, the quality drivers of reds out of Te Mata,' Buck explains.

The aspect of both vineyards is northerly, with a slight eastern tilt. Behind them, Te Mata Peak provides shelter from the southerly source of Hawke's Bay's cold weather. Their easterly inclination admits early-morning sunshine to the vines, accelerating temperature rise – a daily process enhanced by the sloping land – all of which works toward high maximum temperatures. This heat is a central issue for Te Mata, as their key red variety is cabernet sauvignon, and even in Hawke's Bay's relatively warm climate it needs every possible heat advantage to get fully ripe.

Having confirmed that the land certainly held the potential, Te Mata began the long and expensive process of developing a vineyard estate which would supply consistently high quality fruit. BDM and Awatea were completely renovated and replanted with new, higher-quality clones of the necessary grape varieties, and within a short time so too was Coleraine. Once these were established, new vineyards were added. The first was at Ngatarawa, where Peter Cowley and his family are shareholders in the Bullnose vineyard, to which another vineyard, Isosceles, has been added in the same district. At Woodthorpe on the Tutaekuri River an even larger viticultural development will ultimately see 120 hectares under vine, as well as a new winery, separate from Te Mata Estate, to process most of them.

The Bordeaux theme permeates them all. The red varieties cabernet sauvignon, cabernet franc and merlot are planted at all sites, and while the best results at Havelock North come from cabernet sauvignon, merlot seems to perform better at Ngatarawa. Sauvignon blanc, especially Cape Crest, a dry, oak-tempered style, is performing well at Woodthorpe, as is chardonnay, which is also a success at Havelock North, where the foundation for Elston is grown. Syrah is another which seems to suit Ngatarawa conditions best.

TOP: John and Wendy Buck.
ABOVE: Winemaker, Peter Cowley.

Vineyard management is intensive, with a degree of plucking and tucking in all vineyards, along with crop thinning and, at Ngatarawa and Woodthorpe, irrigation. There is no general regime in the vineyard other than vigilance and developing specific solutions for individual sites and conditions, aimed at vine balance in support of maximum flavour intensity and good health. All vines are grafted, and all harvesting is done by hand.

For all the value of having a site with a track record, for chardonnay as well as the Bordeaux varieties, most of Te Mata's vineyards are very young and have no wine history at all. This makes all viticulture part of a long-term development in search of a mix of varieties suited to the various Hawke's Bay conditions within the estate. Aside from the Bordeaux classics chardonnay and sauvignon blanc, there are a number of other varieties which have been added to the mix in recent years. Most prominent is syrah, which has performed well since it was introduced in 1997, and experiments are continuing with viognier and gamay noir at Woodthorpe.

The winery, too, has been transformed since Buck and Morris took over, with dedicated white wine and red wine sections, impressive new barrel-storage facilities, office suites, a laboratory, and sales and tasting area now forming a complex that is a fine example of industrial/rural design. There is a new-world attitude about the buildings, yet their form and the manner in which the winemaking is facilitated around a central courtyard have a strong flavour of France, and particularly of Bordeaux, affirming where the company's philosophy has been lodged since it was established.

Woodthorpe Terraces: expanding the winegrowing base.

'Everything we do is pretty much the way it has always been since we got here. I have always said how the fundamentals of making Bordeaux style reds are simple,' says Buck.

So there have been 20 years of adjustments to the original premise, but no dramatic shifts in any direction. Some of the details which have been refined include increased attention to gentle processes throughout the winery, to ensure every nuance provided by the vineyard is retained in the bottle. For this reason the new red wine fermentation room is fitted with overhead walkways and pneumatic plungers to facilitate easy and regular submersion of the caps on fermenting wines.

It is an important stage, for tannins, matured as fully as possible on the vine, are essential to the structure, flavour and longevity of the wines. Working the cap is a key process. The pneumatic solution came after exhaustive research and visits by Cowley and Buck to various premium wine producers in North America and France.

Barrel craft, too, has been refined, with top wines spending up to 20 months in new or part-new 225 litre barriques. But this fine tuning is done within the parameters of each variety, and each vineyard batch, now in the winery in barrel. Cabernet sauvignon, merlot and cabernet franc all fit into the general pattern: they are crushed, fermented, oak matured, racked, blended and bottled. Their individual characteristics, and those imparted by the vineyards in which they were grown, will call for slightly different treatments in each case, but the process remains fundamentally the same.

'Take the three weeks on skins,' says Peter Cowley. 'We have always left the skins in for three weeks, which is the Bordeaux approach. Over the years we have become much better at tasting wine with the skins in, and we have noticed that at between 18 and 22 days the fruit and tannin balance are just about dead right. Well, we haven't changed, but we sure know why we do it now, and that's pretty much the case right through the winery.'

'..Not necessarily big wines, but aromatic and complex with the ability to age.'

Chardonnay has changed, however, and is probably the wine which has developed most since the eighties. There is now less concern for cautious, reductive winemaking and more confidence in letting the natural process take its course, allowing in more oxygen, looking for texture and richness as much as fruit excitement. Oak remains a major com-

Ian Athfield's architecture extends the notion of cosmopolitan elegance beyond the wines into the fabric of the winery.

ponent, and malo-lactic fermentation has a role to play, depending on the vintage; but there is less measured application of the various components, and more waiting to see what will happen, while all the time keeping a watch by chemical analysis and by regular tasting for evaluation and direction.

Tasting as a winemaking tool is critical to the management team at Te Mata. Buck and Cowley are almost the perfect team; they have both served as competition judges, and Buck trained in London where he acquired a European tasting perspective. Cowley's grounding was initially in restaurants, and then in the academic environment at Roseworthy Agricultural College in Australia. He brings a scientific consideration to Buck's cosmopolitan assessments.

'Our perspective comes from our palates. This has been of huge importance to Te Mata: knowing what we are trying to do, the taste of what we are trying to make. And what we are aiming at keeps getting harder. Every year when vintage is over we have got to start thinking how we can do it better next time,' Buck says.

The composition of all wines is decided in a final process of taste, evaluation and blending that the French call *assemblage*. For red wines such as Awatea and Coleraine, as many as 30 different wines will be assessed for quality, and then for character and specific blending contributions. Single-variety wines such as Bullnose Syrah and Elston Chardonnay will be barrel tasted and selected by quality and character to achieve the desired standards and styles.

With *assemblage* being such an important part of the winemaking process, it is not surprising that the largest obvious change in the process at Te Mata was to cease making single-vineyard wines, as had been the case when the first Coleraine was made. Until the 1991 vintage, Coleraine was produced solely from John and Wendy Buck's Coleraine vineyard opposite the winery, while Awatea and Elston were grown on those specific

vineyards. But from that vintage on, Coleraine became a style of wine, the deepest and richest of the Te Mata range, with the accent on bottle age potential. Awatea, by comparison, is more fruity and fragrant, with less richness on the palate and more obvious appeal. Both are blended from and can draw on cabernet sauvignon, cabernet franc and merlot fruit from any of the company's three vineyard areas.

'In order to make top wine you have to expand your blending options. Good as our vineyards here are, there is no such thing as a perfect site, because each has its strengths and weaknesses. By spreading yourself across many options you will get better, more consistent wine,' Buck argues.

This is, of course, the Bordeaux position, but it is also the mark of a commercially minded wine producer, which Te Mata is. Wine quality aside, the company is obviously successful and extremely profitable, which makes new projects like Woodthorpe not only possible but also a logical expansion of a commercial formula which works.

It also makes Te Mata one of the few truly grand wine estates in New Zealand, a place which oozes restrained luxury.

'Our perspective comes from our palates... knowing what we are trying to do, the taste of what we are trying to make...'

STONECROFT

HAWKE'S BAY

Wine played very little part in the establishment of Stonecroft. Rather it was an exercise in rationalism, stimulated by the notion that wine was possible, and interesting, and motivated further by Alan Limmer's desire to do something on the land. Unlike many other similar projects which have developed high-quality winemaking cultures, Stonecroft's planning was not influenced by quality standards or styles suggested by tasting premium European or Australian wines; instead it was a process of identifying the fundamentals of high-quality wine production, and using those as the basis for development.

Dr Alan Limmer, an analytical chemist, was in a perfect position to carry out the plan, with his laboratory used extensively by leading Hawke's Bay winemakers to identify the chemical source of problems in their wines, and to help with remedies. What he noted was that the cause of the majority of their problems was in their vineyards and the way they grew their grapes, not in their wineries. It was this which formed the foundation of his own winemaking project.

'The problems winemakers were having then related back to the land. Excessive vigour in particular was setting up imbalances in the vines, which was passed on to the fruit, whether it was ripe or not, and consequently into the wines. If the grapes aren't ripe, you have nothing to manipulate in the winery, and if you have to make a wine in the lab, then basically you are stuffed,' Limmer says.

Having decided on winemaking, his plan was simple: to identify a plot of land where the conditions were suitable for vineyards which would naturally grow high-quality fruit. Having identified excessive vigour as an issue, he was looking for low

FAR LEFT: Syrah

OWNERS: ALAN AND GLENNICE LIMMER

WINEMAKER: ALAN LIMMER

PRODUCTION TARGET: 4,000–5,000 CASES

ALL WINE IS NOW ESTATE GROWN ON 6.5 HECTARES OF VINEYARD, WITH ANOTHER 2.5 HECTARES TO BE PLANTED, IN THE MERE ROAD/ROYS HILL AREAS OF THE GIMBLETT ROAD DISTRICT WEST OF HASTINGS IN HAWKE'S BAY. THE SITES ARE FLAT AND THE SOILS ARE DEEP AND STONY WITH SOME SILT COVERING AND VERY LITTLE WATER-HOLDING CAPACITY. FORTY PERCENT IS PLANTED IN SYRAH, 20% IN CHARDONNAY, 20% IN GEWÜRZTRAMINER, AND THE BALANCE IN CABERNET SAUVIGNON AND MERLOT.

SYRAH WAS THE FIRST WINE TO ATTRACT ATTENTION TO THE WINERY AND HAS SET THE STANDARD FOR A RESURRECTION OF THIS VARIETY IN NEW ZEALAND VINEYARDS IN THE PAST DECADE. IT REMAINS THE HIGHEST-PROFILE WINE IN THE RANGE, CLOSELY FOLLOWED BY GEWÜRZTRAMINER. RUHANUI, A SYRAH/CABERNET SAUVIGNON/MERLOT BLEND, HAS BEEN A NOTABLE SUCCESS, AS HAS CHARDONNAY, ALL BEING FULL-FLAVOURED, RICH STYLES WITH PROVEN POTENTIAL FOR IMPROVEMENT WITH BOTTLE AGE.

'...all the characteristics you find in the wine come from the vineyard.'

fertility and low rainfall throughout the growing season to control vine vigour naturally. He also identified the need for the greatest possible heat in the vineyard during ripening, and local conditions which would secure freedom from the spring frosts which are a risk throughout Hawke's Bay. In Mere Road, west of Hastings, he discovered a patch which conformed to all of the parameters he set in 1982. The soils are very young river shingles with light deposits of silt, and were considered so poor at the time that horticulture of any sort existed only on the fringes. The principal land use, in spite of a handful of new vineyards, denied any horticultural potential at all, and in-cluded a drag-racing strip, the municipal refuse dump, a shingle quarry and a military small-arms range. Its poor water-holding capacity determined that irrigation would be essential for grape growing, but in all other ways it was exactly what he was looking for, and he bought 4 hectares.

Having identified the land, the next project was an analysis of the available grape varieties. In this, at least, an element of emotion tempered Limmer's careful consideration of the avail-able data, as one of his first choices was gewürztraminer, a variety which was producing promising results in the fertile soils of Gisborne but had been unsuccessful both in Hawke's Bay and in Marlborough, where the stony soils were similar in structure to those of Mere Road. His decision was based entirely on his enthusiasm for Gewürztraminer wine, although the other two varieties planted, chardonnay and cabernet sauvignon, were those which had the best track record in Hawke's Bay.

All varieties were sourced from Matawhero in Gisborne, then the most reliable supplier of premium-quality vines for vineyard development, and all were grafted onto phylloxera-resistant rootstock. With SO4 and ARG1 among the only stocks available at the time, and with very little field trial research material available which applied to New Zealand conditions, it was not a scientifically based solution. But it was the best possible.

In 1984, after a nearby grower had success with sauvignon blanc which had been made into wine at Glenvale, a little of this variety was added to the vineyard, along with some syrah which Limmer had taken from the government viticultural research station at Te Kauwhata. Part of the trial vineyard there, syrah had never produced reasonable wine, nor had it performed well for the limited number of producers who had tried it in various New Zealand vineyards during the seventies, so the evidence on the variety was scant and negative. However, given the high temperatures at the Mere Road site, and its low fertility, both of which compared favourably with the conditions in the successful syrah-growing region of Northern Rhone in France, Limmer believed it was a calculated risk worth taking. He also had a hunch that low-vigour viticulture would prove an advantage, and there was certainly scope for experimentation with premium red varieties. Cabernet sauvignon had in general failed to produce a consistently high standard of wine in New Zealand, and in 1984 there was no other red wine variety looking likely.

Since the vineyard was established in 1983/84, very little has changed to the fundamentals of Limmer's approach to wine production at Mere Road. The wines are still based, unequivocally, on the vineyard and the grapes it provides each year.

'Fruit is the prime ingredient, and all the characteristics you find in the wine come from the vineyard. My winemaking is all about honestly reflecting what the fruit offers,' Limmer says.

Some things have changed, most noticeably the extraction of sauvignon blanc during autumn 2001 and its replacement by syrah, because the pressure exerted by Marlborough on sauvignon blanc makes the style of Sauvignon Blanc grown in Mere Road outside market expectations. The success of Stonecroft Syrah has also placed considerable pressure on supplies, and commerce demands it is given a greater share of the vineyard. For the same reasons the area given to gewürztraminer has also increased, and in 1993 another 4.8 hectares of land at nearby Roys Hill was added to the vineyard and is being progressively planted in the established Stonecroft varieties.

Viticulturally, irrigation demanded the greatest attention in the development years to suit the site and the vines' need for a balanced water regime throughout the growing season. It took a number of years to learn the balance between water stress due to induced drought and excessive vigour through over-watering, but that balance was

Alan Limmer and old friend.

achieved in 1990 and has been maintained with relative ease since.

The vineyard naturally produces low crops, on average around 6 tonnes per hectare, and even in a wet vintage such as 1988 there is such little water-holding capacity that production is always controlled by vine training and irrigation. Initially, the vines were all trained to vertical shoot positioning (VSP), and although various different trellis systems have been tested, VSP has proved to be the best for all vines, with the exception of gewürztraminer. This variety's tendency to very leafy canopies, even in a dry, low-fertility site like Mere Road, creates an imbalance between fruit and shoots, giving rise to maturity problems. By using Scott-Henry systems, this is corrected.

Mere Road vineyard – a remarkable lineage of rich flavoured wines.

The infertility and dryness of the site have acted against the vigour-control logic which is behind most of the new trellising systems, and has also worked to make SO4 a much more acceptable rootstock at Stonecroft than many New Zealand winegrowers have experienced. Limmer considers that SO4's drought susceptibility is also an asset, by making the vines particularly sensitive to the irrigation regime and ensuring that water application throughout the season is accurately managed. However, ARG1 has been dispensed with, as it was not fully phylloxera resistant and the continued risk of phylloxera infestation was an unnecessary risk.

By 1990, Stonecroft was established and the experiment, at least in terms of the quality of fruit being grown and the attention being drawn by Syrah and Gewürztraminer, could be considered to have been a success. It was time to reconsider the project, for the winemaking was not as sophisticated as the fruit quality demanded, nor was there much economic future in producing from a mere 4 hectares. Limmer decided it was time to expand the vineyards and winery, and to apply the same rational consideration to his winemaker processes as he had to the vineyard.

Wellington wine judge John Commerfod was employed as a consultant to provide taste evaluations and guidance, regularly tasting at the winery and considering Stonecroft's wines as well as others within an international range dictated by the vineyard's varieties and performance to date. It was a process of sensory evaluation and rationale rather than one of accumulative data and chemical evidence, and from it Limmer deduced a vision of balance and harmony that has since guided all his winemaking at Stonecroft.

'It doesn't matter what the wine is, because vintage will dictate that as much as I will. My job is to make the wines as seamless as possible, to make the wines personable no matter what their character is. The great years will be bonuses, but most years aren't like that, and all you can strive for is that they are in harmony, that they have balance in proportion to the character of the vintage,' Limmer says.

One of the established characteristics of Stonecroft's wines is their emphatic flavour – which is as well, as Limmer won't accept 'wimpy wine'. Even the whites have a robust nature that owes as much to richness of flavour as to aggressive winemaking. In the past there have been a number of winery experiments which have taken the wines to the extreme, but invariably they have had the flavour to support their enthusiasm. Now the approach is more circumspect, and more considerate of the nature of fruit delivered by each vintage.

Malo-lactic fermentation and oak handling are examples of the change. In a high-acid vintage, malo-lactic fermentation will be more extensively used than in a year when the acids are relatively low, and oak treatment is also used according to the relative strengths of individual vintages and batches of wine. Care is always taken to support the fruit, rather than subvert it. Five hundred-litre puncheons are common in the winery, and it is unusual for

'It doesn't matter what the wine is… My job is to make the wines as seamless as possible.'

a wine to see more than 50% new oak.

From the earliest vintages, Stonecroft wines have had a propensity to age well, a feature which Limmer attributes to the vineyard rather than his winemaking. This remains the case, although much more attention is now paid to getting tannins as ripe as possible in the vineyard, and then fine tuning aspects of winemaking like post-fermentation maceration times and cap manipulation. Tannins are considered crucial, but only in the context of the wines.

Indigenous yeasts have also become a key part of the winemaking process, beginning in 1996 and gradually gaining a greater share of fermentation so that they now account for 50% of production. They have demanded Limmer's perseverance, because they tend to be unruly, but they give more intensity and appeal to the wines, and contribute a winery-specific character not otherwise available.

ABOVE: From vineyard to winery, Stonecroft is very much a one man operation.

LEFT: Once an industrial wasteland, this district is now a viticultural jewel.

For a winery with such an impressive reputation, there is a refreshing honesty in Limmer's attitude to his wines and his winemaking. The changes he has undertaken have certainly modified the style of the wines and made them more complex, more sophisticated, but he concedes this has not been a conclusive exercise. Every year will bring new problems, teach new lessons and demand different solutions, which is a long way from the certainty of the original Stonecroft plan.

'I now have a very clear picture of how I want each of the wines to appear out the other end. It's not a particular wine, it's a target. For ten years I went through the motions, but I didn't know what I wanted. Now everything I do is in sync with what I want,' Limmer explains.

His growing reputation among the world's Syrah producers suggests others want it too.

DRY RIVER
MARTINBOROUGH

It was changes to the research culture of New Zealand's scientific community which drove Dr Neil McCallum, a scientist, to wine. But only if wine gave him the chance to pursue the highest international standards without compromise – a chance he believed was possible in the Martinborough terrace district newly defined for its winegrowing potential by his compatriot Derek Milne. After applying due intellectual rigour to Martinborough's prospects, Neil and his wife Dawn decided to take the family to Martinborough and make the move to winegrowing. They considered they could survive happily, and succeed creatively, with a small, quality-focused vineyard and winery producing around 1,000 cases of wine.

That was in 1979. Two decades later the promise has been substantially realised in a winemaking pedigree which has few peers in New Zealand, and which has attracted international attention for the quality of its wines. Each year's releases are sold out within weeks, and the prices charged are, across the range, the highest of any New Zealand producer. It is a dream realised, and with surprisingly little adaptation to the fundamentals applied originally to winegrowing and production, with the single exception of commerce. Dry River now produces more than twice the planned amount of wine, much to the delight of its supporters, although their satisfaction has not been McCallum's principal consideration here.

'We felt we could live off 12,000 bottles a year, but the tax laws kept changing, the Government kept wanting more of our capital, and to survive we have had to expand,' he says. He also notes that their success would not have been possible without a supportive market of enthusiastic and generally well-informed wine drinkers who have grown in sophistication with the winery, and who have been prepared to pay good prices for its wines.

Of the rest – viticulture and winemaking – McCallum's research was

LEFT: Pinot noir.

OWNERS: NEIL AND DAWN MCCALLUM

WINEMAKER: NEIL MCCALLUM

PRODUCTION: 2,500 CASES

TEN HECTARES OF OWN VINEYARD ON THE MARTINBOROUGH TERRACE, WITH ANOTHER 2 HECTARES OF ARAPOFF VINEYARD LEASED.

ALTHOUGH TINY, DRY RIVER HAS BEEN AN ENORMOUSLY INFLUENTIAL WINE PRODUCER ACROSS VIRTUALLY EVERY ONE OF ITS VARIETIES AND WINE STYLES: PINOT GRIS, GEWÜRZTRAMINER, RIESLING, CHARDONNAY, PINOT NOIR AND SYRAH. IT HAS FREQUENTLY SET STANDARDS OF HIGH QUALITY FOR THE REST OF THE INDUSTRY AND INVARIABLY CHALLENGED OTHERS WITH ITS UNEQUIVOCAL PURSUIT OF A CERTAIN STYLE AND ATTENTION TO DETAIL.

Sold-out and closed, the normal situation at Dry River.

exhaustive before he began, and there is little he would change if he began today in the same situation. Commerce again suggests that there would be no sauvignon blanc in the vineyard, as its flourishing trade has narrowed the scope for winemaking expression and limited its profitability, moving its commercial status close to the commodity category.

At the root of McCallum's wine philosophy is his palate experience. He points out that the source of Martinborough's ultimate success was not its much-vaunted winegrowing potential but the small tasting group of Wellington scientists who coalesced around Danny Schuster's enthusiasm in the early seventies. Schuster – winemaker, consultant, pioneer and oeno-missionary – attracted an inquisitive set of minds to the process of evaluative tastings, stimulating interest into a quest for excellence which has found its expression in Martinborough. Members of this group took their wine enthusiasms on an exploration of possible winegrowing locations in the vicinity of Wellington, discovered Martinborough and developed it as a winegrowing district in which many of them, like McCallum and Derek Milne, continue to be key participants.

Evaluative tasting remains the basis of Neil and Dawn McCallum's winemaking direction and standards. Every day since the early seventies they have drawn corks on wines which are considered to be international benchmarks, tasting and considering what it is that defines their character and quality, becoming familiar with the established culture of wine excellence.

Initially Neil's palate suggested that pinot noir was not the certainty in Martinborough that others claimed, and when the first Dry River vineyard was planted there was no pinot noir. Pinot gris *petits grains* vines sourced from the Society of Mary vineyards in Hawke's Bay; sauvignon blanc from Matua Valley in Auckland, where Ross Spence was leading development with this variety; and gewürztraminer from Matawhero in Gisborne, already acclaimed in the seventies as the finest producers of Gewürztraminer wine, were the original selections.

The sources for each of these varieties indicated just how careful McCallum was in his research and development, settling for only the best available in each case. He also left half the vineyard without wine-producing vines, working on the assumption that what he and others would learn by growing grapes in Martinborough would be more informative than anything he could discover from research based on other winegrowing areas. So he put half the vineyard into rootstock vines, giving time for consideration of the questions he had about pinot noir and chardonnay, yet providing the opportunity to develop a vineyard of each more quickly through field grafting than by beginning with new young vines. The rootstock planted was 5BB, deemed unsuitable by the Ministry of Agriculture and consequently unpopular with the wine industry on the grounds that it was too vigorous. However, according to available data from Germany where the vine was developed, it seemed more suited to Martinborough than the available alternatives, so McCallum went with it. He remains more than happy with his decision, although 5BB continues to be rare in New Zealand vineyards.

Particularly pleasing have been the results from pinot noir on 5BB. Dry River's field-grafting programme began in 1987 after it became more certain that pinot noir would do well in Martinborough. At the same time McCallum was persuaded that the chardonnay clone best suited to his conditions and expectations was Mendoza, so this and pinot noir clone 10/5 were grafted onto the 5BB roots, followed by clone 5. Recently a mixture of the newly arrived Dijon clones has been added in the interests of complexity, and all are dry farmed as has been the standard in the vineyard since the beginning.

This commitment to dry farming is also at odds with the accepted norm in Martinborough and throughout New Zealand's drier east coast vineyard regions, where drip irrigation is standard practice. McCallum argues that Martinborough receives enough moisture during the growing season to sustain the vines, although only if crop levels are kept very low. Because he has identified restricted cropping as one of the essentials of fine wine production, with maximum crops of 6 tonnes per hectare, dry farming does not present a problem at Dry River, and it serves, as McCallum says, to remove the temptation to 'pump up production levels to please the bank manager'. It is interesting to note that in very dry years, Dry River's vineyards appear to perform better than surrounding irrigated vines, but McCallum is quick to point out that this is only a cursory observation, not the result of careful research of the two systems. Nevertheless, he remains convinced dry farming has been one of the key elements in his wines' performance.

One change in the vineyard was the adoption of Scott-Henry trellis systems under the influence of viticultural scientist Dr Richard Smart. Dry River had begun leaf plucking early on, even though the problem of heavy canopies was less extreme in Martinborough

Neil McCallum, 'One of the turning points as a winemaker is when you realise you can and should be different'.

than in other winegrowing regions. Scott-Henry seemed to be a solution, but it proved to be less effective than the old-fashioned vertical shoot positioning (VSP) under a strict canopy maintenance regime. Smart had identified the problem in general terms; McCallum subsequently solved it in his own specific vineyard environment by reverting to a modification of the traditional standard. Decisions are always based on tangible results, not process, and with tasting as his guide it is in the vineyard that McCallum makes the decisions which shape the style, character and quality of his wines.

'The big changes I make to concentration, ripeness and richness happen in the vineyard. There are always vintage-to-vintage changes which force certain things – decisions such as whether to allow botrytis in or out, and how long to hang on to crops before they are just right. Flavours, structure, tannins are all made in the vineyard. If I didn't have total control there I would be in trouble,' he says.

Control, and an inquisitive energy which obliges him to consider any and every option which may pass his mind – including the unusual one of reflective mulch. This development of Kumeu-based researcher Jonathan Toye, who was working to eliminate bitterness from persimmon crops, involves using a special fabric covering on the ground beneath the vines to enhance ripening conditions. As well as advancing maturity across all varieties, it has proven to be effective in ripening the stalks of pinot noir bunches – essential in the development of structure and rich textures in the wines.

Not that innovation for its own sake is attractive to McCallum. His winemaking approach from the beginning was traditional, but always strained through his own definitive ideas based on exhaustively reached conclusions. He sees answers as being far more complex than first appearances would suggest, and uses as an example the conflicting attitudes in Europe and New Zealand to sulphur levels in wine. Europe's premium producers make their wine to be left for at least five years before drinking. This makes high sulphur levels not just acceptable but a part of the process of producing wine to age well. Conversely, New Zealand wine, even at the highest-quality levels, is bottled and drunk young, and anything other than purity of flavour is unacceptable – a situation enhanced by the natural clarity of fruit flavour in New Zealand wines. The difference, Neil McCallum asserts, is not technical, but cultural.

'There are a lot of things we don't understand at first glance. Not everything is

LEFT: In the winery an intense attention to detail.

Vineyard innovation with reflective mulch.

production based, because the consumer has an influence, too. Then we have to think things through and connect them to the consequences if we are going to get our winemaking right,' he says.

As a natural product of Martinborough-grown grapes, fruit purity is an important part of Dry River wines, but as a corporate ingredient rather than the focus of attention. Anaerobic techniques which secure that fruit factor are important in the winery, although they have been refined to accommodate the demands of texture, richness and harmony that drive McCallum's quality expectations. There is also, he believes, the role of personality beyond that of vineyard or variety.

'One of the turning points as a winemaker is when you realise you can and should be different. But you shouldn't deviate for the sake of it; you must respond to the differences of your region, but how far you take them is up to you,' he says.

McCallum has always sought to build structure, to make wines which age well. This is obvious in all his wines, with even Sauvignon Blanc having a propensity for bottle development that is unusual. But it is the Pinot Noirs which make the strongest declaration of his different winemaking approach. McCallum's Pinot Noirs have about them a quality that is unique in New Zealand, and that the French term *vin de guarde* – a deep-seated reserve that invites bottle age to release their locked-in richness – although there has been a move towards more firmly structured styles. At Dry River ripe stalks are a central issue, and there has been a dual evolution in seeking vineyard solutions to structural questions, like reflective mulching, as well as to those in the winery, like whole-bunch fermenting. It is a process of balancing the feel of the tannins within the character as well as the structure of the wines, to fit structure with texture and, significantly, richness.

There is also the matter of oak, of introducing it in such a way that its presence is clearly felt but is never overt in either Chardonnay or Pinot Noir. Subtlety is the Dry River way here, a definitive attitude delicately delivered, reflecting Neil McCallum's caution about artifice in wine, and his aversion to dependence on an inflexible recipe which prescribes how everything is to be done.

For all the exhaustive research, perpetual inquisitiveness, analysis and attention to detail, Dry River is a high-risk business, its primary role being to manage uncertainty. Intervention in the vineyard is positive and meticulous, yet the dry farming method leaves much to nature and the vagaries of vintage. More than once the vineyard risks have been almost too much for this little producer, yet the natural ebb and flow of vineyard and winery are left to their own dynamic energies at crucial stages of the process, and remain the key to Dry River's culture.

Superficially, Dry River is simply founded on taste and the fundamentals of premium wine production – low cropping and naturally balanced winemaking – and this remains much as it was at the beginning. There is, however, a sub-level at which control is the key: every attention to detail has been refined over successive vintages, moving inexorably towards McCallum's ideal. He will probably never reach it.

Straw bales waiting for mulching.

ATA RANGI

MARTINBOROUGH

Ata Rangi's story is an extremely personal one. Founder Clive Paton is one of Martinborough's hard core, the small band of believers who responded to Derek Milne's positive report on the potential of the Martinborough terrace as a winegrowing area. Including Stan Chifney, the McCallums at Dry River, and Derek Milne, Duncan Milne, Claire Campbell and Russell and Sue Schultz at Martinborough Vineyard, this group created a fine wine enclave out of a small, isolated sheepfarming community which lacked any sense of wine or a wine culture. Certainly the social environment was not sympathetic to high-quality winegrowing, a complication which made their plans alien even where the physical potential was tantalising.

Clive Paton himself came to wine by an unusual route, via dairy farming and a business as a 50/50 share milker. It was not so much a career, although the land and its trees were always immensely important to him, as a means to an end. The dairy industry offered a chance of good profits which he could then apply to a land project rather more exciting than milking cows. Wine was a possibility, for he had a strong interest which Milne's report stimulated, and he determined to take a look. In the course of his first day in Martinborough he was convinced, and on the spot made the decision to plant a vineyard and become a winemaker.

It was not a decision taken lightly, nor without well-informed consideration of the difficulties nature would enforce along the way.

'I was lucky, I came from the land so I knew exactly what risks agriculture posed, and what climate was all about. I knew the scale of the chal-

FAR LEFT: Pinot noir in summer, close-planted next to the winery.

OWNERS: CLIVE PATON, PHYLLIS PATTIE, OLLIE MASTERS AND ALISON PATON

PRODUCTION: 10,000 CASES

ESTATE VINEYARDS OF 18.2 HECTARES ON THE DEEP, LIGHT, SHINGLY SEDIMENTARY SOILS OF THE MARTINBOROUGH RIVER TERRACE, PLUS A FURTHER 12 HECTARES UNDER LEASE OR LONG-TERM MANAGED CONTRACT.

THE CLIMATE IS DRY AND COOL AT THE BEGINNING AND END OF THE SEASON; ALL-SEASON COLD SPELLS ARE POSSIBLE FROM SOUTHERLY CHANGES, AND FROST IS ALWAYS A DANGER IN SPRING AND AUTUMN.

HALF OF THE VINEYARD IS PLANTED IN PINOT NOIR, THE BALANCE IN CHARDONNAY, SAUVIGNON BLANC AND PINOT GRIS, WITH A SMALL AMOUNT OF SYRAH, MERLOT AND CABERNET (FRANC AND SAUVIGNON).

THE OUTSTANDING WINE HAS BEEN PINOT NOIR, AND CHARDONNAY HAS SUBSEQUENTLY EMERGED AS A WINE OF SIMILAR STATUS. CÉLÈBRE, A RED BLEND BASED ON CABERNET, AND A PINOT NOIR ROSE MAKE UP THE RANGE, WITH SOME SAUVIGNON BLANC AND PINOT GRIS.

lenge,' Paton says.

He bought the land in 1980, and in a typical wine community technology share spent the following vintages working at the Auckland wineries of Abel's and Delegats, learning the basics before applying himself to his own wines. It was a short apprenticeship, but from the first vintages there was enough in the wines to give Paton confidence for the future. Nonetheless, it would be a considerable time before the business would be as successful as the wines, or before Martinborough would accept its new winemaking persona.

The first vines planted were based on the assumptions in the Milne report and Paton's vision of being a specialist, against the trend of most wine producers at the time. Pinot noir, gewürztraminer and cabernet sauvignon were planted, although only cabernet prompted any particular interest for Paton as a wine: Australian and French Cabernet Sauvignons or Shiraz were his preferred styles. That was until 1982, when he tasted a French Burgundy which changed his attitude completely.

'It was a bottle of Chambolle Musigny. I can't remember the producer or the vineyard, but it was a seminal wine for me. It was outstanding quality, with a balance of silkiness and depth that I had never seen before in any red wine, and have rarely seen since,' he remembers.

He planted his vineyard according to the standard New Zealand layout of the time, with 1.5 metres between rows, the rows 3 metres apart, and with post-and-wire trellises and vines trained to vertical shoot positioning (VSP). The vines he bought from the best available sources, but although cabernet sauvignon has been relatively successful as a constituent part of Ata Rangi's Célèbre wine, the stand-out variety since the early days has always been pinot noir. Gewürztraminer was soon dropped, because initially the wines were never impressive enough for Paton and it performed so erratically it was never sufficiently commercially reliable to persist with. It was Pinot Noir which impressed from the beginning.

Part of Pinot Noir's performance at Ata Rangi can be attributed to

Clive Paton, 'I was lucky, I came from the land...'

the original clone that was planted. Otherwise known as the 'Abel' clone because it was originally planted by Auckland pinot noir pioneer Malcolm Abel in his Kumeu vineyard, Paton calls it the 'Gumboot' clone because of its colourful history. Abel apparently came on the cuttings when he was working as a Customs Officer and discovered them secreted inside a pair of gumboots in the luggage of a traveller returning from Europe.

The smuggler's story was that he had 'jumped over the fence' at Romanée-Conti in the Burgundy village of Vosne-Romanée, and taken the cuttings from the most exclusive pinot noir vineyard on earth. A good story, and judging by the character of the wines they have produced at Ata Rangi, it could just be true, for it has always been the principal contributor to their Pinot Noir wines, and until 1990 it was the only one.

As more experience of viticulture was gained, and the culture of fine winegrowing in Martinborough evolved, so did the influence of viticultural experts such as Dr Richard Smart. His research into the effects of vine canopies was changing the way New Zealand grew grapes for wine, especially among new, information-hungry producers like Clive Paton.

Team Ata Rangi – Brittany Paton, Nessie Paton, Clive Paton, McKenzie Paton, Phyll Pattie, Alison Paton, Oliver Masters, Miller Paton-Masters.

'As soon as Richard muttered anything we were into it,' Paton observes. Scott-Henry trellis systems were quickly adopted, and a variation known as Smart-Dyson was also considered. However, it soon became clear that Martinborough vineyards did not have the sort of vine vigour problems that made Scott-Henry an efficient form of canopy control, and Ata Rangi has reverted to VSP.

They have also found that reducing the number of buds laid each season, and working to keep the vine canopies as open as possible, improves the health and flavour of all

varieties. Paton's experience at Ata Rangi also suggests that vine management is about the spaces in the vineyard as much as it is about working on the actual vines, and the estate vineyards are being progressively moved to closer planting on 1.9 or 2 metre rows with 1.5 metre spaces between vines.

The system is not fixed, however, and Paton is aware that they are still at the beginning of an extremely long project. Chardonnay has been added to the estate vineyards, and since 1989 it has made up an increasingly significant portion of the winery's annual production. 'Gumboot' pinot noir has been joined by various new clones, including clone 5, clone 6 and most of the Dijon clones, all of which make important contributions to the vintage-by-vintage consistency of the Pinot Noir, as well as to palate complexity. The basis of the Pinot Noir remains the 'Gumboot', however, and is likely to remain so for the foreseeable future.

Of the popular clone 10/5 Paton remains unconvinced, pointing out that the French have tried it and found it below standard. Some 10/5 can contribute to Ata Rangi Pinot Noir in some vintages, but it has not been planted in Ata Rangi vineyards, being sourced from independent vineyard blocks which the company manages. However, this status is merely current, not absolute, as the learning process continues each year, triggering more revision of techniques, adjustments, fine tuning and the development of an Ata Rangi style that is responsive to its particular set of conditions and vintage range.

'The learning that goes into vineyard sites is constantly changing. Young plants are different from 10-year-old plants, and then another 10 years on it's different again, and so are the wines they produce – different concentration, different tannins. You need a lifetime to understand it all.'

It is a similar situation in the winery, which began specialising in red wines made with a minimum of fuss in the safest possible way. Over time this has evolved, with greater risk-taking and experimentation based on both the lessons learned and the invaluable experience gained by the international version of technology sharing – visits to France to absorb another winemaking culture. There have been specific technical gains from this process, but the greatest advantage has been immersion in a process which is substantially fixed by the length of its history, the depth of its knowledge. Living and working in such conditions provides as much confidence as it does technical and artisan

LEFT: Pinot noir in winter, close-planted next to the winery.

skills: a confidence to experiment.

In the winery this has seen the introduction of techniques such as cold soaking, the use of indigenous yeasts and whole-bunch pressing that are innovative to Martinborough but are traditional in many parts of Burgundy. These are then adapted according to the Martinborough experience, which is naturally different from the French.

Of these, cold soaking and indigenous yeast fermentations remain important parts of the process, but whole-bunch pressing was stopped in the 2000 vintage because of the element of hard, green characters it introduced to the wine. This could be a consequence of unripe grape stalks which are more common on mature fruit in Martinborough than they are in Burgundy. The learning process continues.

With Chardonnay, too, the Burgundian influence is considerable, with the target being Meursault's style of rich fruit and oak balance with supportive texture. Chardonnay is also a measure of the personal changes which have transformed Ata Rangi in the nineties. The person responsible for Chardonnay is winemaker Ollie Masters, who with his wife Alison Paton became a shareholder and active proprietor of Ata Rangi in 1995. What had begun as a one-man vision has become a family venture that is quite unique in New Zealand winemaking.

Clive Paton was single when he began Ata Rangi, and when Phyllis (Phyll) Pattie became his partner in 1987, she also became his business partner, bringing her own winemaking skills to the company. Formidable skills they were, too: it was Pattie who established Ata Rangi's Chardonnay credentials with a series of smart wines in 1989, '90 and '91. To this cultural expansion Clive's sister Alison added an extra dimension. She had been supplying grapes to Ata Rangi from her own neighbouring vineyard, and with her husband Ollie Masters an obviously talented winemaker as well, there seemed to be

'We must maintain our determination to learn... because we know we are at the very beginning here. What we do is the key to the future.'

potential for a role-sharing, extended-family operation. In 1995 the company was changed into a four-way partnership, with Clive Paton, Phyll Pattie, Ollie Masters and Alison Paton each holding 25% of the shares.

Responsibilities between the four seem to have split comfortably into areas which suit the disposition of each. Clive Paton has retained his red winemaking and responsibility for the vineyards on which it relies, while Masters is in charge of whites, with Chardonnay his special project. Pattie manages administration, and uses her winemaking skills when required, while Alison Paton handles the critical area of sales and marketing on which the whole operation, and the two families, depend. Their children keep the winery and its satellite family homes lively.

The relationship between the four seems to be a new antipodean version of the great family-run European wine estates, but with a particularly New Zealand character – laid-back efficiency. It gives Ata Rangi a charming sense of conviviality and quiet purpose, as well as a casual hedonism that is perfectly suited to a family making fine Pinot Noir and Chardonnay.

In four equal minds there is also a great capacity for the sensory evaluation on which the winemaking standards are based. Regular tasting of their own and other wines is the key to understanding what their target is, as well as to identifying mistakes and flaws. But most of all, with children running around between vine rows and barrels, there is a sense of continuity in the place.

Pinot noir leaf

'We must maintain our determination to learn,' says Clive Paton. 'That is not only what keeps it interesting, it also keeps us honest because we know that we are at the very beginning here. What we do is the key to the future.'

MARTINBOROUGH VINEYARD

MARTINBOROUGH

Wairarapa's modern history began with a report on Martinborough prepared in 1979 by Dr Derek Milne, a soil scientist with the Department of Scientific and Industrial Research. This report identified similarities between the soils and macro-climate of the Martinborough district in southern Wairarapa and those of a number of the world's leading winegrowing regions, notably the Côte d'Or in Burgundy. The conclusion was that Martinborough had the physical attributes essential for growing high-quality grapes for winemaking, and among the varieties identified as being suitable was pinot noir.

That document attracted a lot of attention among Wellington's community of wine enthusiasts, and become the foundation for the establishment of Martinborough's vine-yards. It was also the catalyst for Derek Milne, his brother Duncan and his wife Claire Campbell, along with friends Russell and Sue Schultz to establish Martinborough Vine-yards, their own project aimed at turning the research into reality.

The stimulus for their venture was more specific than fine wine, more specific even than Martinborough: it was pinot noir and the prospects this variety held for a red New Zealand wine which would attract international attention. It is an idea put succinctly by the company's general manager Paul Shortis, embellished a little with the advantage of hindsight.

'What they saw was an opportunity to do something different. They saw that it was possible to make great Chardonnay in a lot of places in the world, or to make great Cabernet Sauvignon. It was also possible to make top Sauvignon Blanc, but why compete with Marlborough? Pinot Noir not only looked interesting, it was also a chance to do some-thing special in the wine world,' he says.

FAR LEFT: Winery buildings grow almost as quickly as the vines in Martinborough.

OWNER: PRIVATE COMPANY. SHAREHOLDERS INCLUDE DEREK MILNE, DUNCAN MILNE, CLAIRE CAMPBELL, RUSSELL AND SUE SCHULTZ AND WHAREKAUHAU COUNTRY ESTATE.

WINEMAKER: CLAIRE MULHOLLAND

PRODUCTION: 8,000 CASES

TWENTY-ONE HECTARES OF VINEYARD ON THE ALLUVIAL SOILS OF THE MARTINBOROUGH TERRACE. LIGHT LOAMS WITH DEEP, FREE-DRAINING, SHINGLE-BASED STRUCTURES SITUATED ON AN ANGLED TERRACE TILTED TOWARDS THE HUANGARUA AND RUAMAHANGA RIVERS TO THE NORTH AND WEST GIVE THE SLIGHT SLOPE A NORTHERLY ASPECT.

THE CLIMATE IS DRY THROUGHOUT THE GROWING SEASON, AND THE TEMPERATURES WARM, AS HIGH AS 35°C IN FEBRUARY. FROST IS A SPRINGTIME PROBLEM OWING TO THE PROXIMITY OF MOUNTAIN RANGES TO THE WEST AND SUSCEPTIBILITY TO COLD SOUTHERLY CONDITIONS. TEMPERATURE RANGE BETWEEN WINTER AND SUMMER IS MODERATELY CONTINENTAL, WITH AN AVERAGE VARIATION ON THE MEAN OF 25%. THE DAILY RANGE DURING THE GROWING SEASON IS APPROXIMATELY 11.5°C.

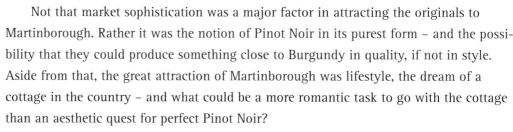

PINOT NOIR HAS BEEN THE WINE WHICH HAS ATTRACTED MOST ATTENTION, AND IT HAS CONSISTENTLY BEEN CONSIDERED AMONG NEW ZEALAND'S FINEST RED WINES SINCE THE LATE 1980S. CHARDONNAY, SAUVIGNON BLANC, RIESLING AND GEWÜRZTRAMINER, AS WELL AS RARE EXAMPLES OF BOTRYTIS-INFLUENCED SWEET WHITES FROM VARIOUS VARIETIES, HAVE ALSO ENJOYED AS MUCH CRITICAL ACCLAIM AS THE ILLUSTRIOUS PINOT THROUGHOUT THIS PERIOD.

Larry McKenna, 'I had been raised on Australian reds... so I had to learn everything. I was starting from nothing, really.'

Not that market sophistication was a major factor in attracting the originals to Martinborough. Rather it was the notion of Pinot Noir in its purest form – and the possibility that they could produce something close to Burgundy in quality, if not in style. Aside from that, the great attraction of Martinborough was lifestyle, the dream of a cottage in the country – and what could be a more romantic task to go with the cottage than an aesthetic quest for perfect Pinot Noir?

But the reality of winegrowing and production demands more of its participants than romance, and after the first awkward steps culminated in a wine which was more interesting than impressive, it was time to find a winemaker who could lead the quest. One of the few they interviewed was an Australian then working for Delegats in Auckland, Larry McKenna, who was as unsure about Pinot Noir as they were but had a confidence to match theirs.

'The biggest challenge was realising how significant Pinot Noir was. Seeing the future back then was not easy for anybody, and when it came to Pinot Noir I had hardly any experience even drinking it. I had been raised on Australian reds from shiraz and cabernet, so I had to learn everything. I was starting from nothing, really,' McKenna remembers.

The paucity of support among the originals in Martinborough accentuates just how tenuous pinot noir's claim was. Although the Milne report attracted risk-takers, only two were prepared to invest in pinot noir – Martinborough Vineyard and Ata Rangi. This was not really surprising, as all experiments with pinot noir up to this stage had been disappointing, and there was nothing conclusive in the Milne report to persuade sceptics. Milne's data did suggest that there were similarities between Martinborough and Burgundy, but they also showed that there were as many differences – soil being the most obvious, as well as the continental climatic effect, wind influence and rainfall pattern. Add this to the abundance of experience around the new world that pinot noir was a most difficult variety to acclimatise outside of Burgundy, and the surprise is that there were any prepared to back pinot noir at all.

The programme from then on was high risk, although a degree of caution appropriate for a new winegrowing region was obvious in the fruit-salad selection of varieties initially planted: chardonnay, gewürztraminer, riesling and sauvignon blanc as well as pinot noir. The proof of the project's success could be measured by the wines made from these varieties at Martinborough Vineyard, with every one gaining the respect of winemakers and critics around the country for their quality. But pinot noir is where they have set their own standards.

Initially it was a case of learning how to grow pinot noir successfully, rather than making it in the winery. This was a completely different approach from the then standard winemaking practice of performing miracles in the winery on fruit which was less than perfect. Many of the techniques originally applied to get any sort of performance out of pinot noir have subsequently become accepted methods for all premium wines.

'Pinot noir is more sensitive than any other variety, and we had to find out everything as we went. As the only ones taking it seriously, there wasn't anywhere in New Zealand we could go and learn, and trial and error with such a hard variety is risky. The first lesson in handling pinot is that you learn a hell of a lot about vineyards,' says McKenna.

The original pinot noir vines were the 10/5 clone, but now the vineyard boasts a diverse range of clones including all the UC Davis and Dijon versions, with Bactobel one of the few that is not represented. McKenna adopted the eclectic view early on, convinced that clonal variety not only gave a range of flavour components but also hedged against variation in vintages. Whatever the climate, there was a chance one of the clones would find conditions to its liking.

Detailed viticulture is the standard regime at Martinborough now, and after some experimentation with various trellis and pruning techniques the company has settled on vertical shoot positioning (VSP) as the best for Martinborough conditions. As there is no serious vigour problem with any of the pinot noir clones in the vineyard, they have decided that the rigorous canopy systems offer nothing to their wines, and VSP is a more efficient use of vineyard labour, and produces results as good as, and usually better than, the alternatives. VSP also allows more air movement at ground level, which can be valuable during periods of high frost risk.

Claire Mulholland: confidence and a rare skill with detail.

Frost is a major issue in the district, and there is a large budget for helicopter use each year. Flying a helicopter over vineyards threatened by frost does limit the damage, and in many cases actually prevents frost from forming by keeping the air moving and pushing cold air away from the vines. It is an expensive contingency, but one which successful Pinot Noir has the financial capacity to afford.

'The target has always been to produce world-class Pinot Noir, and we have been lucky to have the market for Pinot Noir grow at the same time we have appeared. The western world's baby-boomer generation are more wine aware than any before them, and they are interested in new ideas and are prepared to pay for high-quality wine. Right now they want good Pinot Noir, and without them we could not be viable,' says Shortis.

Which is another way of saying that the commercial future is in Pinot Noir, and of explaining why some of the original varieties have been dumped after high-class performances. Gewürztraminer and sauvignon blanc, in spite of producing some very high-quality wines, have been replaced with pinot noir as the demand for the wine increases supply pressure and forces up prices. Chardonnay survives as a perfect and traditional white partner to Pinot Noir, and recently some pinot gris has been added to complete the market mix.

McKenna likes to understate the influence of winemaking on the development of Martinborough's Pinot Noir style, but his contribution has been immense. In the winery the exhaustive series of trials he ran from 1986 to 1999 to test the options for every detail, from clonal and rootstock selection to yeast, bacteria, maceration and oak maturation, have provided the evidence for Martinborough Vineyard's style and the speed with which their Pinot Noirs reached a consistently high standard.

More than this, McKenna has been the catalyst for the whole Pinot Noir movement in New Zealand. His activism on Pinot's behalf, and his own burgeoning expertise, are acknowledged by other leading Martinborough producers as a major reason for the district's current status. Through the annual Pinot Noir workshops which he fostered, he has generously shared his knowledge around the country, and has encouraged others to do the same, improving national standards to a level totally unexpected a decade ago.

At the heart of this attitude is a genuine feel for the value of community, and his own experience of learning in France. After a handful of Martinborough vintages McKenna

LEFT: The commercial future is in Pinot Noir.

'The first lesson in handling pinot is that you learn a hell of a lot about vineyards.'

visited Burgundy to work through the vintage of 1990, and returned with what he believed was the essence of making good Pinot Noir. It was something he already suspected.

'I had to go to France because I couldn't really claim to know anything until I had been there and experienced Burgundy. What I found was that we knew all the winemaking techniques, knew the science, we just needed to get the details right and we couldn't learn that – that's experience. What it did teach me was that good wine is all about the vineyards. That is where the French excel,' he says.

McKenna has since left Martinborough Vineyard to pursue other pinot noir options, and a new generation of Milnes and Schulzes have taken their seats at the boardroom

table. The legacy of the original vision has been realised in a Pinot Noir reputation which is second to none in New Zealand. It is now in the hands of new winemaker, with more vineyards, a greater portion of pinot noir, and a corporate structure clearly intent on a rich international future.

'Our real competitive advantage is Pinot Noir. Larry's legacy is still here and carries on under Claire Mulholland, and we intend maximising that. Our current development stage will take another five years, at the end of which we will be selling 9,000 cases of Pinot Noir out of a winery total of 14,000 cases. We started as a very entrepreneurial company with faith in Pinot Noir, and we still are,' says Shortis.

'We started as a very entrepreneurial company with faith in Pinot Noir, and we still are.'

NEUDORF

UPPER MOUTERE, NELSON

Neudorf is unusual among New Zealand's winemaking successes, because it was established at a time and in a place when there was little knowledge of the grape-growing requirements of fine wine production outside the principal winegrowing regions of Auckland, Hawke's Bay and Gisborne. When Neudorf was established late in the seventies, the whole of the South Island was virtually unknown territory for winegrowing: Marlborough's vineyards were not yet a decade old, and there was no winemaking experience within 300 kilometres to draw on. It is true that Nelson had a history of earnest enthusiasts who had made some fairly rustic wines, and Herman Seifried had proven that grapes could be grown successfully at Upper Moutere, but there was no evidence that anything other than subsistence viticulture could be successful in the region. Of the prospects for making wine of real quality, nothing at all was known.

'Wine knowledge was pretty basic,' remembers Tim Finn. 'I got the wine bug tasting and talking about wine with the guys at the Te Kauwhata (Viticultural) Research Station. Wine then was an introduction to a wide range of possibilities, and the sense that in New Zealand we could realise them. We had great self-belief, and self-determination, and it offered to fulfil a lot of the things we wanted to do. It took us back to the land, but it wasn't milking cows – it was out there, enjoying the wider world.'

Rather than being daunted by the prospect of starting something completely new – they were unsure of the exact winemaking process, and unsure what varieties to plant or how to plant them – Tim and Judy Finn were excited by the idea, by the challenge of coming to an new area, of not knowing what wine would demand of them.

The only options available were to take a large gamble on a couple of varieties and hope for the best, or to try everything. The second choice was the

OWNERS: TIM AND JUDY FINN

WINEMAKER: TIM FINN

PRODUCTION: 15,000 CASES

NINE HECTARES OF HOME VINEYARD, 4 HECTARES LEASED IN MOUTERE DISTRICT AND ANOTHER 8 HECTARES AT BRIGHTWATER. THE HOME VINEYARD IS PLANTED IN CHARDONNAY AND PINOT NOIR, WITH A SMALL TRIAL OF PINOT GRIS.

THE STANDOUT WINE SINCE THE MID 1980S HAS BEEN CHARDONNAY, WITH RIESLING AND SAUVIGNON BLANC SHOWING THE SAME ELEGANCE AND FINESSE. RECENTLY PINOT NOIR HAS EMERGED AS A WINE OF SIMILAR STYLE AND QUALITY.

LEFT: Mendoza clone chardonnay.

'Wine knowledge was pretty basic...'

least risky, and the original Neudorf vineyard had a fruit salad of varieties: müller thurgau, chenin blanc, semillon, cabernet sauvignon, pinot noir, sauvignon blanc, merlot, cabernet franc and gewürztraminer, as well as breidecker and five or six other Geisenheim varieties. For a small, 5 hectare block this was an enormous range, but it was an essential trial to find exactly what would grow successfully in the Moutere clays of sunny north-west Nelson. And even then, there was a chance none would succeed.

But this was part of the spirit of scientific exploration that appealed to Tim Finn, along with pioneering experience of starting something completely new. There was support from people like Herman Seifried who had begun his own Nelson experiment in 1974, and from Lincoln University where the first experiments in establishing a tertiary wine training and research department were being established. But their experience was only marginally better than Finn's own, and the biggest problem, says Finn, was, 'We didn't know the questions to ask.'

So it became learning by doing, and a number of lessons were gleaned from the first few vintages, beginning in 1982. Most of them were difficult – and primarily the problem was fruit quality. Although some interesting and promising wines were made – enough to gain national attention in the bright and tiny new world of experimental New Zealand wine – the signs were obvious that progress would be negligible unless the issue of fruit quality was addressed.

The required information came from viticultural scientist Dr Richard Smart. Early in the eighties Smart, an Australian, was employed at the Agricultural Research Centre, Ruakura, where his research into canopy management and enthusiasm for his results changed New Zealand winegrowers' attitudes to viticultural management. By altering trellis systems on which grape vines grow so as to limit the amount of leaf canopy supported by the vines, Smart showed how fruit quality in traditionally managed, fertile New Zealand vineyards such as those at Moutere could be transformed. According to Smart, the traditional, heavy vine canopies limited leaf and grape exposure to sunshine and warmth, restricting ripening and cropping levels. It was the break the Finns needed. Employment of Smart's ideas at Neudorf transformed their grape quality, and they remain the foundation of the winery's quality programme.

'In the end growing grapes is inseparable from making wine. We do a lot of work in the vineyard, clipping, trimming, tucking, and that is the basis of it all. You are not going to make good wine from bad fruit, and we will make very good wines no matter what we do in the winery because the fruit is right,' says Finn.

Even prior to Smart, it was already obvious at Neudorf that some grape varieties from the fruit-salad selection they were growing showed potential while others were definitely not worthy of long-term support. Chardonnay showed potential from the first vintage, and by 1986 revealed the elegance and warmth which are its hallmarks, in spite of the herbaceous characters typical of poor vineyard management. Gradually all the vinifera hybrids such as müller thurgau and breidecker disappeared, along with semillon and chenin blanc and most of the reds, cabernet sauvignon, cabernet franc and merlot. Neudorf wasn't their place, and as chardonnay became increasingly successful and marketing demands asserted themselves, so did varieties such as sauvignon blanc which were doing relatively well in Moutere conditions. Without a reduction in value or quality, these could be sourced from elsewhere in Nelson, or even from Marlborough, but chardonnay had become a speciality of the hard, stony clay soils of Moutere.

Rosie, Judy and Tim Finn.
(Photo: Craig Potton)

By trial and elimination, the vineyard, now grown to 9 hectares with a judicious purchase of neighbouring land, is almost exclusively chardonnay and the ugly-duckling variety which survived against the odds, pinot noir. The first pinot noir planted was the upright clone 22, which had been successful as an appealing, fruity light red in the early days but was destined to be less than suitable for Neudorf's rapidly developing reputation as a premium producer of Chardonnay. Yet for all its lack of colour and short life, it had a character which intrigued Tim Finn, and he stuck with it, reducing crop levels until it produced wines serious enough to demand further attention. It became clear that pinot noir was a candidate for the future, and new plantings of 10/5 pinot noir were made to develop this wine further, along with more recent additions of the newer Dijon-sourced pinot noir clones. Yet clone 22 remains, and will always make up a substantial portion of Neudorf's vineyards simply because it continues to offer Finn that certain something

'The fun and essence of winemaking are the differences offered by separate sites...'

which attracted his attention at the beginning.

Both pinot noir and chardonnay are now subject to tight pruning to restrict their cropping to levels similar to those of premier Burgundian vineyards, as the lesson has been that production levels are reflected in quality, and lower is invariably better. Throughout the growing season there is also an intensive regime of canopy management which pays attention to maturing grapes that will contribute to the desired structure and character of each wine.

Winery developments lagged behind those in the vineyard throughout the eighties,

when the issue of fruit quality demanded attention, but the changes in winemaking during the nineties were as dramatic as those in the vineyard. The approach of Tim Finn was also significant here, and it differed from the predominant culture in the New Zealand wine industry at the time. His concentration was on viticulture because he has always believed in the pre-eminence of the land over the lab, an attitude based as much on his romantic inclinations as it is on his experience as a science graduate and farm advisor for the Ministry of Agriculture. While bigger companies were being directed by winemaking and food-technology issues, Finn was wholeheartedly focused on viticultural

A special place where abundance seems to seep from the soil.

solutions.

It is an attitude reflected in Neudorf's labelling, where vineyard sources are prominent. Neudorf Moutere Chardonnay and Moutere Pinot Noir are the flagship wines, without any further classifications of premium or reserve status. Now with the company involved fully in other vineyards in Moutere, as well as at Brightwater, these names will be featured and their differences promoted. It is not, claims Finn, a qualitative decision, as that is fundamental to all the wines they make, but merely one of character.

'The fun and the essence of winemaking is the differences offered by separate sites. The reality is that when you get to make really good wines you can have wines that are different but equally good. There is just as much enjoyment in exploiting those differences as there is in blending for a theoretical super wine,' he says.

The winery changes have been equally significant in developing Neudorf's acclaimed style, particularly with Chardonnay and Pinot Noir, as both demand intensive winery attention after all the work in the vineyards is completed. The first development of Chardonnay was attention to barrels. Finn decided on small, 225 litre French oak and fine tuned the barrel fermentation component so that it harmonised with the natural elegance of Moutere-grown Chardonnay. Finn was also quick to embrace the concept of lees contact in an effort to improve the texture and richness of the wines, and the fine tuning of this process has continued, invariably being moderated according to the character of each vintage. Winemaking, viticulture, does not take easily to fixed management standards, and a degree of flexibility is demanded by the natural fluctuations of the growing and fermentation process. The only certainty is that every year is different.

And every variety. Riesling, which has been a notable if less publicly acknowledged success for Neudorf, demands less winemaker attention and more effort to maintain its fruit purity. Conversely, Pinot Noir is in many ways more delicate and demanding even than Chardonnay, and the process towards similar standards of quality has been longer and more challenging. Oak is essential here, but so is the development of tannin structures which are suited to red wine but not detrimental to Pinot Noir's sensitivities.

The truth is that the experimental regime at Neudorf continues. New vineyards demand new solutions in the winery as much as they do in the vineyard, and only Chardonnay has a track record at Moutere that can be called a definitive pedigree. Naturally, changes with Chardonnay are more subtle than they are with Pinot Noir, or with the new experiment, Pinot Gris.

From the beginning, however, Tim Finn's touch in the winery has been certain, and it invariably contributes to Neudorf's reputation for elegant wines. The real change has been in his learning how to manage his Moutere vineyards to grow the quality grapes his winemaking demands.

Marketing has never been especially difficult for Neudorf because their production size has always been smaller than their reputation, even as the national wine culture has flourished around them. Yet in the office as well as the winery the business has always had an air of professionalism in the way Tim and Judy Finn have conducted their marketing and corporate affairs. It may be a romantic venture, but it is based on sound economics.

Early on, the Finns embraced and stimulated the notion that wine offered a social experience greater than that which already existed, and developed their attractive vineyard location to include casual yet excellent food. Now their wine community is an international one, but its roots are deep in Moutere clay.

'We now have a network of contacts around the world, based on the ability of this little place to be part of the world pattern of premium wine,' says Finn. That ability has been discovered and enriched by the Finns' contribution.

A style unequivocally rural New Zealand.

CLOUDY BAY

WAIRAU VALLEY, MARLBOROUGH

Instrumental in the establishment of two of Australia's most illustrious modern properties, Cape Mentelle and Taltarni, David Hohnen was already a leader of the Australian wine renaissance when he was attracted by New Zealand. Coming from an Australian industry noted for its parochialism and its patronising attitude to New Zealand, Hohnen's venture into the still unproven region of Marlborough in the 1980s was remarkable, but it has been justified by Cloudy Bay's phenomenal ascent to its present stellar status as an international brand. Thanks to Hohnen's crisp strategic mind and winemaker, Kevin Judd's equally sharp winemaking, Cloudy Bay has become the most famous New Zealand label, one which has added a definitive gloss to the image of New Zealand wine in the world's most cosmopolitan wine markets.

Founded on a Sauvignon Blanc that expresses the natural purity of Marlborough fruit character, Cloudy Bay remains a vibrant expression of Hohnen's original interest in New Zealand viniculture. The story is that Hohnen was shown a bottle of Sauvignon Blanc by a group of New Zealand winemakers who were visiting Western Australia, and he was immediately impressed by the character and quality of its fruit. 'Penfolds 1983 Sauvignon Blanc from Marlborough just blew me away. It was a bit sweet, but it had fruit characters we would never get in Australia,' Michael Cooper quotes him as saying.[1] Coming to New Zealand in 1984 to explore further he concluded that Marlborough held the potential for serious development, and he determined to establish a winery at the top of the South Island, in spite of the negative response he knew he would get back home in Australia.

FAR LEFT: The Richmond Range beyond the vineyards: inspiration for Cloudy Bay's famous label.

OWNER: FRENCH CHAMPAGNE HOUSE VEUVE CLICQUOT.

WINEMAKER: KEVIN JUDD

PRODUCTION: 90,000 CASES

ONE HUNDRED AND FORTY HECTARES OF VINEYARDS IN WAIRAU VALLEY IN THE RAUPARA ROAD, BRANCOTT AND RENWICK DISTRICTS. GRAPES FROM GROWERS ARE ALSO USED IN ANNUAL CRUSH.

FIFTY PERCENT OF PRODUCTION IS THE WORLD-FAMOUS SAUVIGNON BLANC, 25% IS IN THE PELORUS BOTTLE-FERMENTED SPARKLING WINE, AND THE BALANCE IN HIGHLY REGARDED PINOT NOIR, CHARDONNAY, RIESLING AND GEWÜRZTRAMINER.

TOP: Winemaker, James Healy.
ABOVE: Founder, David Hohnen.

On the same trip he met winemaker Kevin Judd at a wine show. Judd, born in England, raised and trained in Australia, had attracted attention since his arrival at Selaks in West Auckland where he had seen that company's wine quality transformed in one vintage. His Selaks Sauvignon Blancs were notably invigorating and pure, and his laconic approach was not dissimilar to that of Hohnen himself. A deal was done, and by the time the finance, production arrangements and vineyard plans were in place, Judd was on board as Cloudy Bay's first, and so far only, chief winemaker.

Cloudy Bay was established primarily as a premium Sauvignon Blanc producer, with a determination to make the best possible wines in what were then substantial quantities for a wine industry committed to a role as beverage wine producers. From the first vintage, 1985, 200 tonnes of grapes were crushed, establishing Cloudy Bay as a company that had the industrial ethos to compete with premium international labels from Europe and North America. Evidence of its business accuracy and cosmopolitan flair were to come later with innovative (for New Zealand) marketing in sophisticated design and emphasis on a single wine. The labels not only deviated dramatically from the corny, imitative designs typical of New Zealand wine labels, but immediately set standards of sophistication and clarity in an industry which was still marketing wines with generic labels like 'Chablis'. Similarly, the notion that Cloudy Bay was one label, one wine, without a forest of sub-brands and alternatives, was extremely unusual in a marketplace where local wine producers had traditionally made everything from liqueurs and pre-mixed cocktails to Cabernet Sauvignon.

Not that Cloudy Bay was restricted to Sauvignon Blanc; this just was, and remains, their principal focus. Cabernet sauvignon and chardonnay were part of the original portfolio, and although chardonnay has continued to grow in importance, both as a source of single-variety dry white and bottle-fermented sparkling wines, cabernet sauvignon was eliminated within a decade as it failed to perform, never quite losing the hard green edges which are a result of immature fruit flavours. Phylloxera delivered the hardest viticultural lesson of all, however, decimating the company vineyards and those of important growers within a few years of its discovery in Cloudy Bay's own vineyards in 1989, just three years after planting. The vineyards had to be re-established, a drain on capital but an opportunity to revisit other issues like that of cabernet sauvignon.

Fine tuning the vineyard has not always been so dramatic, but as lessons have been learned about growing in a new location like Marlborough, developments have steadily changed the nature of viticultural management, the area where Kevin Judd asserts most of the wines' character and quality are established. After initial experimentation with a number of trellising systems, most of Cloudy Bay's vineyards are now trained to Scott-Henry, and the ongoing programme of canopy management is in place to ensure the vines are in balance and producing peak-quality fruit. One of the principal characteristics of Cloudy Bay, unusual for a premium, vintage wine producer, is the winemaking focus on consistency of style from vintage to vintage. This poses huge problems for the winemaking team, and puts even more pressure on leaf plucking and careful selection of crops that will constitute the final blend.

As with premium quality winemaking from Champagne to Chateaux Margaux, the range of sites available to the winemakers is crucial to consistency and high quality, giving variety of choice in blending from various sites and ripeness options. It also offers early quality control and contributes a level of character complexity in the final wine that is not available to single site producers. In most vintages there are at least 30 different Sauvignon Blancs from which the final blend will be shaped.

Soil is a key to flavour and character differences in the Wairau Plains district of Marlborough where Cloudy Bay is based, and is influential in the strategic planning of viticulture at Cloudy Bay, not just in the range of available wine characters for Sauvignon Blanc, but also in the location of each individual variety. Most sauvignon blanc is grown in the Raupara district where the winery is located, on soils which are predominantly stony. Pinot noir is planted at Brancott, where there is a deeper soil covering to the stones, and more clay, which gives better consistency and more even ripening. Chardonnay occupies a variety of sites in both these and other locations around the region in order to achieve complexity of flavour detail.

Not that viticulture presents the total picture of Cloudy Bay's processes, as each of its wine styles demands a separate winemaking culture. Effectively there are three wineries: one producing large quantities of precisely tailored Sauvignon Blanc; one making more evolutionary, diverse styles of Chardonnay, Pinot Noir, Gewürztraminer and Riesling; and a third producing bottle-fermented sparkling wines. That all are done with the same high

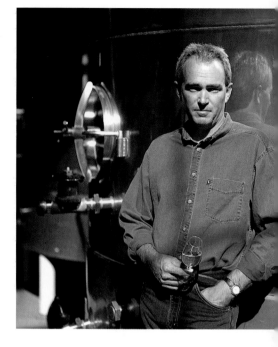

Kevin Judd, winemaker, Managing Director. (Photo: Steven La Plante)

standards and cosmopolitan style is a rare and impressive feat of wine processing.

The sauvignon blanc crop is all machine harvested, as speed is a critical factor once the exact level of ripeness has been achieved in the vineyard: in the cool, minimal-humidity conditions of Marlborough autumns, grapes are left until the last possible moment, and then must be taken quickly and efficiently. As sauvignon blanc is, by comparison with other grape varieties, low in phenolics, machine picking offers speed without an unwanted increase in astringency. The wine is cool fermented in stainless steel, retaining all its natural fruit clarity, although a small batch is aged in oak to contribute another degree of complexity, before it is fined, blended and bottled.

Cloudy Bay has been active in the development of bottle-fermented sparkling wines, a style which Hohnen quickly identified as an option in Marlborough because of the deep flavours and relatively high acidity of its grape crops. In 1986 he invited the Californian sparkling wine expert, Harold Osborne to visit Cloudy Bay and give a judgement on the sparkling wine potential of the region, which was favourable enough to bring Osborne back in 1987 to establish the parameters by which the wine named Pelorus is now produced. Osborne created a style based on Marlborough fruit clarity in the varieties pinot noir and chardonnay. It is subject to the full range of sparkling winemaking craft, with extensive malo-lactic fermentation of the base wines, a 3-year period of bottle maturation on yeast lees, and, as with the Sauvignon Blanc, a good range of blending options. The intention was to produce full, rich wines with strong yeast autolysis characters to balance the bright fruit and fresh character of the raw material. In the process experience has been gained in handling malo-lactic fermentation under Marlborough conditions which has had subsequent benefits in developing Chardonnay and Te Koko.

Viticulture for the sparkling wines is essentially the same as for the single-variety, still wines, although the selection process is targeting different characteristics in the vineyard. With the introduction of non-vintage Pelorus made predominantly from chardonnay, there is a determination to grade chardonnay for the two styles, with the non-vintage lighter and creamier than the vintage.

There are many similarities between Sauvignon Blanc and Pelorus production, not least in their potential scale, although constrained by the capital demands of bottle aging Pelorus remains small by comparison with Sauvignon Blanc at Cloudy Bay. The other

LEFT: Autumn colours in Matthew's Lane vineyard.

wines, some still at a developmental level, demand more individual attention although there is a shared family culture in their access to machine harvested fruit and complex blending options. Their evolutionary nature, and the market expectation of vintage variation in wines such as Pinot Noir and Chardonnay, make them less amenable to the philosophies of consistency applied to Sauvignon Blanc and bottle fermented sparklings.

The first Cloudy Bay alternative to Sauvignon Blanc which attracted public attention was Chardonnay a wine which reflects vintage more surely at Cloudy Bay than Sauvignon Blanc does. Initially chardonnay was not as successful under Marlborough conditions as sauvignon blanc, and more adaptation of viticulure and winemaking has been required to meet its challenge. Significantly a substantial portion of the crop is hand picked, and 20% – 30% of new oak is a feature, with the refinement of oak handling a notable aspect of the style's progress, which, along with development of malo-lactic fermentation and lees stirring has delivered more texture and richness to the finished wine. Most wines now have around 50% malo-lactic content and half of the fermentations use indigenous (wild) yeasts. These techniques serve to moderate the tendency of Marlborough-grown Chardonnay to lean flavours and overblown alcohol – problems which were apparent in early Cloudy Bay wines but have been effectively eliminated.

Pinot Noir represents the greatest developmental change in both viticulture and winemaking at Cloudy Bay, driven primarily by the enthusiasm and commitment of winemaker James Healy. In spite of early difficulties with the variety, pinot noir held the promise of a red wine with elegance and in a style more suited to Marlborough than was the case with other reds. Attention to viticulture has been paramount, partly due to unsatisfactory early clones, and the original 10/5 and Bachtobel clones have been replaced, mostly with clone 5, with a small section of clone 6, and recent additions of the new Dijon clones. Intensive viticultural management and strict crop control aimed at balance and prime fruit maturity are essential, with

Sauvignon blanc.

6 tonnes per hectare the maximum production, for which crop thinning at veraison is important. As with chardonnay, most grapes are hand picked, but machines are ever an option, and de-stemming is deemed important because the stalk tannins in Marlborough fruit to date have rarely been mature enough for inclusion. A cold soak is followed by a short, hot fermentation that is just finishing as the wines are moved into barrel for the final stages. Oak makes a large contribution to the process, with the wines currently spending almost a year in barrel before final bottling.

Kevin Judd describes the Pinot Noir process as being early in its evolution, with some way to go before the wines fully satisfy Cloudy Bay's expectations, but they have already attracted considerable critical attention and are used as evidence that Marlborough's red future is with Pinot Noir. Other innovations which are raising similar signposts for Marlborough's future are the oak-influenced, wild-fermented sauvignon blanc known as Te Koko, a vigorously flavoured Gewürztraminer and a Late Harvest Riesling produced when vineyard conditions suit, perhaps four years in ten.

Although Cloudy Bay is now part of the French Champagne house Veuve Clicquot Ponsardin, a commercial culture into which its sophisticated wines and public persona fit with ease, decisions remain with Hohnen and Judd. Their success permeates the atmosphere at Cloudy Bay's understated, industrial-cool winery, but so does the calculated enthusiasm which created the place and continues to surface in new projects such as Pelorus, Te Koko and Pinot Noir. There is a feeling within the New Zealand wine industry that the development of Pinot Noir has made Cloudy Bay the perfect example of New Zealand's winemaking future, qualitatively and commercially.

Mustang vineyard, Brancott Valley.

1. Cooper, Michael, *The Wines and Vineyards of New Zealand* (4th edition), Hodder & Stoughton, 1993, p.154.

SERESIN

RENWICK, MARLBOROUGH

Although born in New Zealand, Michael Seresin's parents were European, and his own career in the international movie business is decidedly cosmopolitan with a European accent. He has homes in London and Tuscany as well as in the Marlborough Sounds, and is just as likely to be in North Carolina as he is in Sydney, so there should be no surprise in the sophisticated nature of his winery venture, nor its focus on exporting most of its production. What is surprising is that Seresin sees his development in Marlborough as not just a return home, but as a place where he can continue to engage the world at large, to be cosmopolitan while confirming his New Zealand persona.

'My business in film is based in the Northern Hemisphere but I travel constantly in both hemispheres. I was born in New Zealand, love its landscape, wines and people, speak its language and in certain ways feel at home there. I also believe that Marlborough's potential as a wine region and all that encompasses on a local and worldwide scale is phenomenal,' he says.

It is obvious, too, that the winery is not just a factory for processing grapes into wine, nor is it a tourist centre for those fascinated by the exoticism of wine. It is a re-sponse to location and the sophistication that wine implies. The olive trees and olive-processing facility are obvious examples of this, as is the cohesive nature of planting on the estate aimed at enhancing the experience of country that a winery offers. But it is the subtle sign at the gate – a hand print on a large rock: no words, no blandishments – and the architecture which confirm a richer cultural dimension at Seresin Estate.

By engaging an architect as emphatic as Ian

FAR LEFT: Classic Marlborough looking towards Waihopai, dry hills, blue skies and vineyards.

OWNER: MICHAEL SERESIN

WINEMAKER: BRIAN BICKNELL

PRODUCTION TARGET: AROUND 45,000 CASES

THE ESTATE IS SITUATED WEST OF RENWICK ON THE FRINGE OF THE WAIRAU RIVER AND IS DIVIDED BETWEEN VINEYARDS AND OLIVE ORCHARDS, 68 HECTARES IN VINES AND 45 HECTARES IN OLIVES, WITH AREAS OF RESERVE SET ASIDE TO MAINTAIN SOMETHING OF THE FLOW AND FEEL OF THE NATURAL ENVIRONMENT. FINAL VINEYARD PROPORTIONS WILL BE 45% SAUVIGNON BLANC, 20% PINOT NOIR, 20% CHARDONNAY, AND THE REMAINING 15% DIVIDED EQUALLY BETWEEN RIESLING AND PINOT GRIS. ALL WINES ARE MADE FROM ESTATE-GROWN FRUIT.

THE SOILS ARE DIVERSE AND, UNUSUALLY FOR MARLBOROUGH, NOT ESPECIALLY STONY, WITH TWO DISTINCT TYPES DIVIDED BETWEEN AN UPPER TERRACE AND A LOWER AREA CLOSER TO THE RIVER. THE TERRACE SOILS ARE PREDOMINANTLY CLAY, WITH SANDY SILT AND GRAVEL ON THE LOWER SITES.

THE MARLBOROUGH CLIMATE IS DRY
THROUGHOUT THE GROWING SEASON, WITH
DROUGHT RISK ALWAYS HIGH AND ACCESS TO
WATER FOR IRRIGATION AN IMPORTANT
FACTOR FOR MOST VITICULTURE. FROST IS
ALSO A RISK DURING SPRING. TEMPERATURES
IN JANUARY, FEBRUARY AND MARCH CAN TOP
34°C AND AVERAGES ARE CONSISTENTLY
WARM THROUGH TO HARVEST. THE AVERAGE
DAILY RANGE THROUGHOUT THE GROWING
SEASON IS REGULARLY AROUND 11°C.

CHARDONNAY HAS BEEN SERESIN'S
HIGHEST-PROFILE WINE TO DATE, SUPPORTED
BY SAUVIGNON BLANC AND, TO A LESSER
EXTENT BECAUSE OF LIMITED AVAILABILITY,
PINOT NOIR.

Athfield to design the winery buildings there was initially an aspect of grandstanding about the project, especially when taken alongside Seresin's profession as a film producer, but the winery is so obviously functional and understated, as well as stylish, that it manages simultaneously to express the artistic bias of its owner, a rural work ethic that is unmistakably European, and the New Zealand landscape.

Not that good architecture implies good winemaking, but it is a positive start and there is a definite functionalism in the vineyards as well, with pragmatic sauvignon blanc the largest variety by far, followed by potential economic stars chardonnay and pinot noir, with trial batches of so far unproven pinot gris and riesling. Winemaker Brian Bicknell concedes that there should have been more pinot noir initially, but the experimental nature of the vineyard demanded as much market certainty as possible, and sauvignon blanc was always going to have markets waiting for it, provided the wine standards were high enough.

Not all the vineyards are grafted, which is unusual for Marlborough as phylloxera is a major problem in the region, but when the land was first purchased in 1992 some planting was done with ungrafted plants. Since then all vineyards have been grafted on either 101-14, riparia gloire, 3309 or SO4.

At first the vineyards also included a range of red varieties, trialled to see if any had the potential to produce red wine up to the standard already established for Marlborough-grown white varieties. It was an eclectic mix, including two which had already been discarded by most Marlborough growers, cabernet sauvignon and cabernet franc, as well as others yet to be confirmed either way: malbec, chambourcin, merlot and sangiovese. It did not take long before Bicknell and Seresin were convinced.

'We knew early on that we couldn't make world-class wines consistently from these varieties. We tried everything, but it was straightforward from the start that they were not going to work, so we went through and top grafted them with pinot noir and pinot gris,' Bicknell remembers.

Conversely, one of the selected replacements, pinot gris, has forced reconsideration purely on the basis of its early performance. Although, like pinot noir, pinot gris is sensitive to cropping levels, it ripens well, is resistant to botrytis and is not liked by birds which can pose serious problems at harvest. Moreover, it produces the sort of structured, deeply flavoured wines Bicknell and Seresin are looking for.

Given the demands of the international fine wine trade, and the characteristic fruit brightness which is considered Marlborough's defining feature, Bicknell considers ripe fruit and low crops are critical if the wines are to have the mid-palate concentration expected by Seresin Estate's customers. Export is already the most important market for the company, and has been since the first vintage, with 60% of Chardonnay production and 92% of Sauvignon Blanc exported after only four vintages, so there is no room for complacency.

As with most wineries intent on quality wine production, meticulous care and attention to detail are essential parts of the management plan. But in such a young vineyard environment, learning and developing a bank of experience of the land are prime factors in the process. Each year new experiences will make more of the need for fine tuning in the vineyards, and in the winery – a fact made apparent by the ongoing experiment with vine spacings in the pinot noir vineyards. There is also the factor of Michael Seresin's vision of what a wine estate should be and its role within Marlborough's physical and cultural environment. 'Michael looks longer term than I do, and he sees that people will still be growing grapes here in 100 years' time,' Bicknell says.

One consequence of this is a commitment to organic viticulture: no insecticide or herbicides, no synthetic fungicides, and even greater attention to the detail of seasonal fluctuations as well as the responsibility to co-ordinate natural resources rather than direct them. Yet for a traditionally trained winemaker like Bicknell, the process has been encouraging, and the only persistent issue is that of weeds in the vineyard.

The vintage at Seresin for all varieties, even sauvignon blanc, begins with hand harvest. All grapes are passed over a triage table where any rotten or unhealthy berries are culled, and chardonnay, pinot gris and sauvignon blanc are whole-bunch pressed. The intention is to develop a style which is based on elegance, length and subtlety rather than obvious fruit. For this reason a portion of semillon is added to sauvignon blanc to give the finished wine more length and to add a measure of complexity from semillon's nettle characters. Bicknell is also searching for some suitable stony vineyard land on which to plant sauvignon blanc to improve the aroma in this wine.

The natural rhythm of the vineyard is continued as much as possible in the winery as

TOP: Michael Seresin.
ABOVE: Brian Bicknell.

well, where there is no refrigeration in the fermentation area. Even the intensive winery craft applied to chardonnay makes minimal use of sulphur, excludes enzymes and is mostly fermented by indigenous yeasts. Only signs of aldehyde will prompt sulphur additions, and most chardonnay will go six months through fermentation, barrel stirring and oak conditioning before it gets a whiff.

Fermentation can be slow with indigenous yeast, which makes up 100% of Reserve Chardonnays and 80% of the standard label, taking as long as nine days to begin and then proceeding very quickly, reaching maximum temperatures of 26°C. Bicknell's

ABOVE: Pinot gris.

LEFT: Seresin vineyard below Mt Riley and the Richmond Range.

Chardonnay intentions are based on the Burgundian house of Leflaive, looking to use fruit for palate texture rather that fruitiness, and with a healthy measure of good French oak and natural complexity drawing on the fermentation process.

The aim with Pinot Noir is similar, although use of different clones in the vineyard provides the core of the finished wine's character. Clone 10/5 provides back palate and structure; clone 115 is favoured for its consistency from vintage to vintage and the richness it produces in the mid palate, with lower acidity and higher pH; while clone 375 gives an attractive floral character. The newer Dijon clones have also been planted, along with a number of Marienfelds and UCD 22, and the process of experimentation continues each vintage.

De-stemming remains important, as there is no evidence so far that the stalks are ripe enough to be included. Four days of cold soak and thrice-daily plunging are followed by week-long fermentation during which daily plunging continues, as much as five times during the hottest period. On completion, the wine is immediately racked into oak, where it will undergo a natural malo-lactic fermentation and regular stirring. Again it is a process of minimal interference, with no racking for 15 months, and no filtration at all before bottling.

All of which can change as the vines get older, as new lessons are learned from new clones of pinot noir, or different vintage conditions place different demands on the winery. What seems unlikely to change is Michael Seresin's attitude to his project, although it is already larger and considerably more demanding than he first expected.

'A wine industry and the endeavours associated with it, like food, music and the arts, have a civilising influence on any culture. I hope that Seresin Estate can contribute to this essential part of life in Marlborough.'

'On a world scale we are seen as a friendly people, a very physical nation with powerful land and seascapes. I believe that the wine world can contribute to an even more diverse and embracing culture,' Seresin says.

ABOVE: 'A wine industry and the endeavours associated with it, like food, music and the arts, have a civilising influence on any culture.'

RIGHT: 'Michael looks longer term... and he sees that people will still be growing grapes here in 100 years' time.'

VAVASOUR

AWATERE VALLEY, MARLBOROUGH

If tradition is a factor in winemaking, then the Vavasour family has a long, if not especially triumphant, wine history, for one of their ancestors was cupbearer to William, Duke of Normandy and King of England, known to the British as The Conqueror. Other than that – and the occasional glass with dinner – the Vavasours of Ugbrooke in Marlborough, station holders and farmers, had no vinous traditions to speak of when Marlborough began to look like a serious winegrowing region and winegrowing became an option for farmers looking to diversify their land interests.

In the mid eighties, Marlborough's wine industry was based on the stony soils of the Wairau Plain adjacent to the town of Blenheim, over the hill to the north of Ugbrooke's situation in the Awatere Valley. However, to Peter and Anna Vavasour there seemed no reason why the similarly stony soils of the Awatere Valley terraces, and a virtually identical climate, could not be used to winegrowing advantage on their own estate.

When consulted on the prospects, viticulturist Richard Bowling not only agreed with them but he also became an enthusiast for the Awatere's potential, especially for red wine. In discussions between the interested parties, a Special Partnership was formed to plant

vineyards on Vavasour land and to develop a winery. Comparisons between Awatere climate data and those of established winegrowing regions in other parts of the world suggested to the Vavasours and Bowling that there were sufficient similarities between their sites and Bordeaux to look to the latter as a blueprint. The plan was established: to make premium, cabernet sauvignon-based reds in the Bordeaux tradition. In 1986 cabernet sauvignon, merlot and cabernet franc were planted, as well as

FAR LEFT: Awatere Valley vineyards dominated by Tapuae-o-uenuku, a warrior from the waka Araiteuru, who turned into a mountain on arrival in Aotearoa.

OWNER: PRIVATE COMPANY
WINEMAKER: GLENN THOMAS
PRODUCTION: 30,000 CASES

A 31.5 HECTARE VINEYARD IN THE AWATERE VALLEY, MADE UP OF 60% SAUVIGNON BLANC, 15% CHARDONNAY, 15% PINOT NOIR AND 10% RIESLING. IT ALSO TAKES GRAPES FROM GROWERS IN THE AWATERE AND WAIRAU VALLEY REGIONS OF MARLBOROUGH.

PREDOMINANTLY WHITE WINE PRODUCERS, WITH TOP-RANGE CHARDONNAY AND SAUVIGNON BLANC, AS WELL AS SMALL QUANTITIES OF RIESLING. PINOT NOIR BEGAN COMING TO THE FORE AT THE END OF THE 1990S.

significant quantities of the variety already proving to be a boon to Marlborough, sauvignon blanc, and some experimental chardonnay and pinot noir.

Another factor was critical to the success of what was always intended to be a very small, quality-focused operation: a winemaker with the skill to turn out wines of the required standard. Peter Vavasour contacted David Hohnen, who had just established Cloudy Bay in Marlborough, and Hohnen's advice was to approach Glenn Thomas, an Australian winemaker who was working for Corbans in Marlborough at the time. Thomas said yes, and he has been responsible for every Vavasour vintage, beginning with the 1989.

Many wine producers who have pioneered a new region discover that innovation is expensive as well as technically risky, especially when the company concerned is small, is building a market and experimenting with new land. Caution is required, yet it is difficult to know exactly what to be cautious about.

'You have to learn quickly. It takes a long time for vines to grow, for wine to be made and for people to taste it, before you can find out what your mistakes are, what your strengths are, and can develop from there,' says Thomas.

Unfortunately, Vavasour's biggest lesson was that their enthusiasm for Bordeaux was not supported by their winegrowing experience. It soon became apparent that neither cabernet sauvignon, cabernet franc nor merlot was suitable for commercial viniculture in the Awatere, much as they have also proved to be unsuited to the Wairau. In very good vintages, good wine was made, but too often it did not develop the full, ripe flavours expected of premium wines. In such vintages, no red wines were produced under the Vavasour label, putting considerable financial pressure on a young company already struggling with the negative cash flows and extreme capital pressure exerted in the early years of wine development. In the mid nineties the decision was made to pull out the Bordeaux reds and concentrate on what the Awatere had quickly revealed as its real potential – chardonnay and sauvignon blanc, with serious possibilities in pinot noir and, later, riesling.

The chardonnay originally planted was entirely of the Mendoza clone, already the preferred selection of all the leading North Island producers. But in Marlborough, and in the Awatere in particular, experience revealed a tendency for Mendoza to develop high

Winemaker, Glenn Thomas, 'Balanced wines are the important thing...'

sugars and acids without full flavour maturity, resulting in big, fierce wines which lacked fruit intensity or balancing richness. In response, Vavasour have planted clone 95 as their principal chardonnay clone, with a little Mendoza going a long way to make the original now a mere 20% of the chardonnay crop. Acid levels, especially malic acid, are now at a manageable level for Thomas.

The other experimental variety, pinot noir, has also proven to be potentially one of the Awatere's best performers, although viticultural developments with the variety have been more demanding and more detailed than with chardonnay. Originally, clone 10/5 was planted, but a wide variety of new clones have been added to the vineyards, and a regime of attentive canopy management throughout the growing season has been developed, more so in sites which are not well suited to pinot noir and could undergo a change of variety in the future. It is becoming apparent that site variety, like clonal variety, is a crucial part of the development of complexity in Pinot Noir wine.

'We have seen quite noticeable variations in pinot noir according to soil around the vineyards, where the range covers gravel and loam and most in between. We find that the more aromatic wines come off lighter ground, for example. You don't have to grow everything on boulders. Balanced wines are the important thing, so we are learning how to make viticulture really site specific and are seeing the results in the bottle,' Thomas explains.

All pinot noir crops are also thinned at veraison, even in the low-cropping Awatere, just to ensure the right degree of concentration and colour. Vineyard work, once in danger of being mechanised, is now more labour intensive, and vine sensitive, than ever.

Judging by the expansion in vineyard area by outside producers, including most of the large North Island-based companies which also have vineyards in the Wairau, Vavasour's Awatere experiment has been extremely successful. Their experience of the distinctive Awatere wine characters emerging from the valley vineyards is also being borne out by these new developments, with flavours more aligned to mineral and flint characteristics than those of their Wairau neighbours.

'These are the characters of low crops with varieties like sauvignon blanc and chardonnay, and the Awatere is less productive than the Wairau. Eight tonnes per hectare is pretty normal for us. With Sauvignon Blanc you don't get that sweaty character, and

Peter Vavasour and his daughter, Claudia.

the wines have more spine, and I think both Chardonnay and Pinot Noir have fine quali- ties,' says Thomas.

Not that Vavasour's wines are exclusively from the Awatere. Growers in the Wairau provide grapes for the company's successful second label, Dashwood, and Wairau-sourced fruit is included in Vavasour wines if Thomas believes such blending produces better quality. The intention is always that Vavasour labels should be the best possible, and if there is no fruit of the required standard in a certain vintage there will be no Vavasour wine made from that particular variety that year.

'Ultimately winemaking here is about producing the best possible wine. The fruit could originally come from a grower, or from our own vineyards: it could be from Awatere or Wairau; it could be from the most expensive barrel, or from lesser, older oak. The point is, why be a pedant? I just want to make the best,' says Thomas.

This is the philosophy behind the Vavasour Sauvignon Blanc label – one of progres- sive selection from the best vineyard sites with established track records for producing riper, richer flavours, through to batch selection from tank and barrel, and then the final blending according to taste and balance. These wines are treated to all the luxury winemaking processes of barrel fermentation and maturation, malo-lactic fermentation and lees stirring, at least in part.

The Chardonnays by comparison are treated with considerably more delicacy, al- though the same degree of selection in the vineyard and winery is apparent throughout. All the chardonnay is hand picked and whole-bunch pressing has been introduced to preserve fruit clarity and delicacy, with the winemaking focus on elegance and fruit intensity. To this end, oak treatments are more circumspect, with only a small barrel- fermentation component, and always in old barrels to minimise the presence of strong young oak flavours and astringency. The change from the early vintages, when up to 70% new oak was used, has been dramatic, with the proportion of new oak now down to 15%. Thomas is also careful to avoid excessive malo-lactic fermentation, partly achieved through the lower malic acid level normal in clone 95 juice. Eighty percent of fermentations are made using indigenous yeast, another development from the total inoculation of the early vintages, and there is a steady programme of lees stirring to impart the required creamy texture.

Above: The Vavasour family cockerel emblem. 'The reality is that you have to build a brand if you want to gain recognition...'

LEFT: Vineyards on the northern side of the Awatere Valley.

'It wasn't a case of copying the Burgundians. It was about finding a way to do it here.'

The delicate approach refined for Chardonnay since 1990 has also been an advantage in the development of Pinot Noir in the late nineties into a worthy substitute for the founders' original dreams of red wine excellence. It is a variety that has always demanded careful and detailed winemaking, more in keeping with white wine than with red, according to Thomas, but even then he admits to greater changes in attitude and technique with pinot noir than with any other variety.

'It wasn't a case of copying the Burgundians. It was about finding a way to do it here. Every year is different, and all the little winemaking details are particular, needing constant attention. A bit here and a bit there is how you change, rather than making dramatic jumps in any direction, and small changes can make all the difference. But all the time we are responding to what we get out of the vineyard, not by heading off in our own direction,' he says.

Ultimately Pinot Noir will make up some 20% of Vavasour's production: a partner to the company's top Chardonnay, with a support team of Sauvignon Blanc, and of Riesling, which has already shown enormous potential, and possibly of Pinot Gris some time in the future. A tight range, which looks rather Burgundian, not Bordelaise, but very much in harmony with what limited Awatere experience has suggested is ideal for there.

Outside the vineyard and the winery, one other thing has changed dramatically: the notion of a perfect little winery.

'The aim was to be small, a boutique concentrating on good wines. But the bottom line didn't turn out to be fantastic at the boutique end. The reality is that you have to build a brand if you want to gain recognition, and building a brand can only be done with reasonable volume,' says Peter Vavasour.

To be viable, production had to expand, and markets had to be serviced with the same level of sophistication as was being applied to viticulture and winemaking. The secondary Dashwood brand, based on the pure fruit flavours which made Marlborough famous, refined by Thomas's true winemaking style, was launched to help cash flow without compromising the Vavasour brand, and has become the commercial engine for the company. After more than a decade of developmental stress, including politicians dumping the Special Partnership legislation, and the failure of the company's government-owned bank – unexpected changes which demanded recapitalisation before the fourth vintage – Vavasour's 20 shareholders can begin to count their blessings.

The Awatere Valley terraces offer a wide range of different sites and conditions.

111

PEGASUS BAY

WAIPARA RIVER, NORTH CANTERBURY

Ivan Donaldson has been enthusiastic about wine for most of his adult life, and as an amateur winemaker, wine traveller, competition judge and wine commentator has been at the heart of Canterbury's wine circle throughout the New Zealand wine revolution. From an early stage he converted his enthusiasm into winegrowing and making experiments near his Christchurch home, and Pegasus Bay is the product of that experimentation and a personal vision of what is possible in Canterbury.

'We had a fairly clear idea of where we were going when we came to Waipara. My 12 year involvement as winemaker at the first vineyard in this area gave me a good feel of what was possible, so we knew what varieties we wanted to plant, and why we wanted to go to Waipara,' Donaldson says.

Fifteen years after the first vines were planted in 1986 the varieties remain the same – sauvignon blanc, chardonnay, semillon and riesling for the whites, and pinot noir, cabernet sauvignon, merlot, malbec and cabernet franc for red. An unusual range, but one which clearly reflects Donaldson's catholic tastes and a traditional British fine-wine palate based on the regional European wines of Burgundy, Bordeaux and Germany. Personality is a key here, clearly expressed by the status of riesling as the largest white variety, in spite of Ivan Donaldson's reservations about its commercial potential. His wife Christine promoted riesling on the basis that they should grow what they loved as surely as they should grow for profit, and it has proven to be an unlikely success.

Working on the basis that temperature and shelter were the two critical factors in Canterbury,

FAR LEFT: A carefully chosen site sheltered from the chilling easterlies.

OWNERS: IVAN AND CHRISTINE DONALDSON

WINEMAKERS: MATTHEW DONALDSON AND LYNNETTE HUDSON

PRODUCTION: 12,000 CASES

TWENTY-EIGHT HECTARES OF VINES PLANTED ON THE SOUTH BANK OF THE WAIPARA RIVER, NORTH CANTERBURY. ALL WINES MADE FROM ESTATE-GROWN FRUIT.

SOILS ARE PREDOMINANTLY LIGHT LOESS AND SAND ON A FOUNDATION OF GLACIAL MORAINE, WITH POOR WATER RETENTION; THERE IS ALSO SOME CLAY, ALTHOUGH NONE OF THE CLAY SOILS ARE CURRENTLY PLANTED.

CLIMATE IS HOT THROUGH THE PEAK OF THE GROWING SEASON, WITH TEMPERATURES REGULARLY REACHING THE HIGH 30'S. DIURNAL RANGE IS ALSO SIGNIFICANT, AT AROUND 12°C IN JANUARY AND FEBRUARY, AND THERE IS A REASONABLE DEGREE OF CONTINENTALITY. RAINFALL IS VERY LOW,

WITH THE PEAK FALLS IN SPRING.

THE LEADING WINES HAVE BEEN
CHARDONNAY, PINOT NOIR AND RIESLING,
WITH THE PREMIUM LABELS 'PRIMA DONNA'
AND 'ARIA' RESPECTIVELY, ALTHOUGH ALL
WINES HAVE ESTABLISHED A STRONG
REPUTATION THROUGH THE LATE 1990S.

Wind machines ever ready for the
challenge of frost.

the Donaldsons' search for vineyard land focused on the Waipara district where there was some protection from cold easterly conditions. General climatic data also pointed to the area as having the hottest mid-summer conditions in the country, as well as a large diurnal temperature range in mid season and one of the few examples of continentality in New Zealand's maritime climate. These factors have long been considered important for varieties such as pinot noir and chardonnay, although the influence has never been quantified.

Having no luck finding suitable land for sale, Donaldson spent months looking for the best possible locale, and when he found it approached the owner to secure a block large enough to establish a viable vineyard.

They settled on an extremely sheltered, north-facing block close to the seaward ranges on the eastern side of the valley, with suitably deep, free-draining soils.

It has proven to be every bit as hot as they wanted, but too sheltered to be free from frost. Not that this came as a surprise – susceptibility to frost is one of the side-effects of a large diurnal temperature range – but it was a risk they were prepared to take in favour of protection from the easterlies which Canterbury experience has shown to be extremely limiting for viticulture.

'We knew we would have a frost problem, but we can control that to some degree. We can't control the sun or the east wind, though,' says winemaker Matthew Donaldson.

One way of mitigating frost damage is to blast still air into circulation patterns that prevent cold air pooling in the vineyards. This is often done by helicopter at Pegasus Bay, and is also performed by static wind machines installed among the vines. This is now essential to grape-growing on the estate, as the warmth that attracted Donaldson has also accentuated the frost problem, with higher early-season temperatures encouraging bud burst as much as two weeks before normal, creating a corresponding increase in frost risk. In these conditions one frost has the potential to wipe out a whole crop and, if severe enough, part of the following season's as well.

Without the sheltering ranges, however, temperatures would never get hot enough to consistently deliver mature grapes, especially among the Bordeaux varieties cabernet sauvignon, cabernet franc, merlot, sauvignon blanc and semillon. These make up a significant proportion of the vineyard, and although the leading varieties pinot noir, chardonnay and riesling are less dependent on high maximum temperatures, they have responded extremely well to them, producing a consistency of flavour and intensity that is rare among Canterbury vineyards, especially with riesling.

All of the varieties were planted on their own roots, a common practice south of Marlborough where there has so far been no phylloxera. Since the first 20 hectares were planted, a large, 4 hectare trial has been undertaken with four different rootstocks and 15 scions in an effort to establish just which combinations are best suited to their soils and climatic conditions, and to the winemakers' flavour expectations.

There were also experiments with trellis systems in the early years, and Scott-Henry has been established as most appropriate for the Bordeaux varieties. For the other three, vertical shoot positioning is the preferred option. An unintended dry farming trial also lasted for the first two years after planting in 1986. Without water because they had come to no agreement for supply, the vines had to survive as best they could, but when 50% of the vines died because of water shortage they had stark evidence that dry farming at Pegasus Bay is too risky to consider on a permanent basis.

Winemaking team, Matthew Donaldson and Lynnette Hudson.

High natural acid and tannin levels are characteristic of all varieties grown on the estate, placing particular demands on the winery to ensure the appropriate balance is achieved, especially with riesling. As a high-phenolic variety with delicate aromas and flavour profiles, extremely gentle handling and minimal pressing is standard in an effort to preserve the finesse expected in high-quality Riesling. Botrytis is also considered an important component in the top Rieslings, and in certain conditions botrytis does strike the vineyard late in the season, so that for the Aria wine in particular riesling crops are often kept on the vines well past normal harvest in search of some infection to add richness, texture and complexity to the final wine. Usually this is used as a complexity in the finished wine, rather than a dominant, high-sugar feature, although some very sweet wines have been made in this way under rare conditions.

High natural tannin levels also put pressure on Pinot Noir which, like Riesling, has the sort of detailed flavour and soft character which is easily compromised by tannin imbalance. All pinot is hand harvested and de-stemmed before pre-fermentation cold soaking so as to limit contact with the tannin-rich stalks. In an effort to restrict tannin levels further the must is separated from gross lees and racked into barrels to complete the last 10% of fermentation, limiting the potential for alcoholic extraction of bitter pip tannins.

The basis for Pinot Noir production here is the widely used 10/5 clone, which the Donaldsons are extremely happy with. It makes up some 70% of the pinot noir vineyard, the balance being 2/10 as well as clone 5 which was top grafted onto underperforming merlot vines, and all of the first- and second-generation Dijon clones. Clonal selection is not considered to be as significant here as it is in many leading pinot noir vineyards, how-ever, with Matthew Donaldson making the point that vineyard and yield are more important for final wine quality than single clones or the clonal mix within the vineyard.

Of all the red varieties, pinot noir produces full, ripe wines most consistently. Merlot revealed early on that it was not suited to the vineyard, although newer merlot clones have been very promising, and the variety has taken over as the predominant contributor to the Bordeaux red blend from the 2001 vintage. Cabernet Sauvignon's disadvantage appears to be its inability to deliver consist-ently rich, mature fruit flavours, even at very low crop levels, although it carries the high tannin and acid levels better than either Pinot Noir or Merlot, and it adds muscularity to the red Bordeaux variety blends. The accent of the Bordeaux red blends has consequently moved in favour of merlot, and there are positive signs in the malbec trials that this variety could also provide a greater contribution in the future.

By comparison, the white Bordeaux varieties produce flavours rich enough to fit comfortably into a warm, complex style which takes full advantage of barrel fermentation of the Semillon component. No sulphur before fermentation for either also helps with texture and palate complexity, as it does with the other major white variety in the vine-

ABOVE: 'Hands on' usually means dirty hands.

LEFT: Vines shrouded in bird netting.

yard, chardonnay.

In spite of the problems many South Island Chardonnay producers have had with the Mendoza clone, owing to high acid and alcohol levels which create unbalanced finished wines, these have not been apparent at Pegasus Bay. All of the chardonnay in the vineyard is Mendoza, all hand harvested; and the processing is relatively relaxed, with barrel fermentation, minimal sulphur additions until as late as possible, lees stirring, a portion of malo-lactic fermentation and mid-term barrel ageing in small oak. Nothing out of the ordinary for a top quality New Zealand Chardonnay. As the only consistently premium-quality Chardonnay grown south of Marlborough, this success indicates the value of the Donaldsons' careful site selection.

As already mentioned, the varietal balance at Pegasus Bay is unusual: classically Burgundian with Chardonnay and Pinot Noir at the top level, alongside a very aromatic Alsatian Riesling. This trio makes a certain sense, given the growing conditions of North Canterbury, and indeed of all South Island regions, but having a Bordeaux counterpoint of Cabernet/Merlot reds and Semillon/Sauvignon Blanc whites highlights the extremely personal character of this producer. It is a family company, with two of Chris and Ivan Donaldson's sons, Matthew and Edward, as well as Matthew's partner Lynnette Hudson fully involved, and throughout the winery and its wines there is a strong sense of individuality.

This is most obvious in the contemporary art work which hangs on the walls of the tasting centre and cafe at the winery, and in the air of privacy that pervades the garden. The arts theme, this time in music, is repeated in the quartet of top labels in the Pegasus Bay range – Aria, Prima Donna, Maestro and Finalé, names which extend the sense of wine as a component in a broader, richer culture than the one which existed before New Zealand had a thriving fine wine industry.

There is also a strong sense of place at Pegasus Bay, one reflected in the company's commercial plan, and its support throughout Canterbury.

'We feel very committed to the local market. Exports for us are an adjunct to our New Zealand sales, and are unlikely to ever be much more than 30% of our production. Export is obviously where expansion will go, but we make wines in New Zealand, for New Zealand palates,' Ivan Donaldson says.

ABOVE: 'Maru' eating Pinot noir at smoko.

RIGHT: Morning mist over the Pegasus Bay vineyard - the view from Mt Cass.

FELTON ROAD

CROMWELL BASIN, CENTRAL OTAGO

When Stuart Elms got the wine bug, he got it bad, and after a lifetime in farming sent himself off to winemaking school at Lincoln College in Christchurch, where he not only gained a good grounding in the basics of winegrowing and production but also met his future winemaker, Blair Walter. All he needed then was a vineyard, and he already knew where that would be.

Winegrowing had been established in Central Otago in the nineteenth century, but the politically induced slump in winegrowing fortunes in the early twentieth century effectively eliminated any commercial potential and all interest in a viable wine industry. It was another 80 years before diversifying land owners looked again at winegrowing in a region noted for its stonefruit. Pioneers like Rolfe Mills at Wanaka, where Elms had a holiday home, and Alan Brady near Queenstown showed during the eighties what the potential of Central was.

The enthusiasm of Rolfe and Lois Mills was a catalyst for many of Otago's modern winemaking enterprises in Otago, just as Brady's Gibbston Valley was an example of wine's commercial potential. They made it obvious that Central Otago could grow good wine and make a profit doing so, and Elms was undoubtedly impressed enough to plan his own venture in the region.

During extensive research undertaken for the massive Cromwell high dam project on the Clutha River, Bannockburn was identified as the warmest district in the Cromwell Basin: a detail of little interest to dam builders, but a significant one for potential viticulturists. Although there were no vineyards in Bannockburn at the time, this was

FAR LEFT: Central Otago is as spectacular as any winegrowing landscape.

OWNER: NIGEL GREENING

WINEMAKER: BLAIR WALTER

PROJECTED PRODUCTION: 14,000 CASES

TWELVE HECTARES OF ESTATE VINEYARD IN THE FELTON ROAD DISTRICT OF BANNOCK-BURN, CROMWELL BASIN, CENTRAL OTAGO. CURRENTLY PLANTED IN 40% PINOT NOIR, 40% CHARDONNAY AND 20% RIESLING. ULTIMATELY PRODUCTION WILL BE AROUND 70% PINOT NOIR.

VINEYARDS ARE PLANTED ON TWO SOIL TYPES: LOCHAR SERIES WHICH ARE LIGHT SCHIST GRAVELS AND HEAVIER WAENGA SOILS OF LOESS WITH FINE SANDY LOAMS AND SOME CLAY CONTENT.

THE CLIMATE IS VERY DRY AND INFLUENCED BY THE RELATIVELY HIGH ALTITUDE (OVER 200 METRES ABOVE SEA LEVEL) AND THE CLOSE PROXIMITY OF ALPINE AREAS WITH PERMANENT SNOW COVER. THE GROWING SEASON IS SHORT, WITH HIGH MID-SEASON TEMPERATURES AND A RAPID DECLINE AT THE CLOSE. DURING THE SEASON THERE IS A WIDE RANGE OF TEMPERATURES

BETWEEN THE DAILY MINIMUM AND
MAXIMUM, AND A SIGNIFICANT FROST RISK
TO ACTIVE VINES IN ALL BUT TWO MONTHS OF
THE YEAR.

FEW WINE PRODUCERS HAVE ATTRACTED
SO MUCH ATTENTION SO SOON AFTER THEIR
WINES HAVE APPEARED ON THE MARKET. OF
THESE, PINOT NOIR IS THE OUTSTANDING
WINE, ALTHOUGH RIESLING HAS ALSO GAINED
CRITICAL ACCLAIM, AND THE CHARDONNAY IS
CONSIDERED ONE OF THE BEST FROM
CENTRAL OTAGO.

evidence enough for Elms, and in 1991 he purchased a block of north-facing slope along Felton Road and progressively planted 12 hectares of it over the following three years.

The planting programme took advantage of experience gained from the established producers, and avoided the experimental blocks of numerous varieties, most of which would fail. Pinot noir was already looking promising in Central Otago – an advantage of its early ripening characteristics – and both chardonnay and riesling were solid choices, although final conclusions about their adaptation in alpine areas are yet to be made. So 40% of Elms' Felton Road vineyard was committed to pinot noir, with commercial considerations allowing for the balance in white varieties: 40% chardonnay, the rest riesling and a small block of sauvignon blanc.

As is common in regions where phylloxera is a distant threat rather than a deadly reality, few of the original plantings were on resistant rootstocks, with riparia gloire and 3309 being preferred. Ten years on, only 30% of the vineyard is on grafted roots, and experimentation continues on the favoured stock for Felton Road's blend of soils and climate.

From the beginning, Blair Walter was an integral part of the project, although his winemaking skills were not required until they first made wine from their own grapes in the 1997 vintage. Prior to that, the crop was sold off to other Central Otago producers. In less than five years from that first vintage, and surprisingly for such a tiny, distant producer, Felton Road's reputation has grown and spread around the world in fine wine circles. The critical consensus is that the fruit quality of its wines is remarkable.

Walter considers this is just the beginning. 'We still don't really know how to grow the grapes well here, or how to best make wine from them,' he says. 'We are learning.'

And learning fast. Already the particular conditions of Bannockburn are being revealed, with the two soil types delivering different fruit to the winery each season. This has given added weight to the winemaking decision to market these wines under separate labels, such as Block 3 Pinot Noir.

Other aspects of the site have also demanded special management attention. Although rainfall is low, when it does come vineyard run-off can be considerable, and the erosion problem becomes a threat to the vines. From the beginning Elms brought his regional experience to bear, and chose to retain existing drainage channels around the site, and to keep them well planted and maintained so that the water would find its natural course down the slope and away from his vines.

Another aspect of these vineyards is that the maximum daily temperatures of 30°C and more are reached at around 5 o'clock in the afternoon in the key ripening months of February and March. With 24-hour temperature range averaging 13°C during this period, mornings are comparatively cold and in need of the earliest sun they can get, while afternoon shadows are not an issue. Consequently east-facing slopes which are open to the morning sun and the earliest possible rise in temperature are the ideal.

Varietal performance has also prompted quick changes. Sauvignon blanc has been removed, and because of its dazzling performance to date, all new plantings are pinot noir. The ultimate aim is for this variety to make up 70% of the winery's annual production.

It is perhaps telling that the first variety picked each vintage is also the most successful: pinot noir, followed by chardonnay. The last riesling comes off the vines around three weeks after the first pinot. This can be extremely late, however, with the longest season so far ending on 7 May, a month when temperatures have been known to drop as low as -9°C in Cromwell. But even in March frost can be a problem before the grapes are fully mature.

Although the vineyards are all planted on 2.5 metre row spacings, with 1.5 metres between vines, these cooler conditions appear to make vine height an issue, especially with chardonnay, and experiments are continuing to discover exactly where to position the fruiting canes for the best ripening results. Neither pinot noir nor riesling appears to be as sensitive, but all possibilities are being considered.

Water is also an issue in such a dry climate, and its management becomes a key issue in growing grapes for high-quality wines. In the initial stages, the aim was to encourage high health in young vines, with good water supply and sound fertilisation. This has now been dramatically reduced, and water demand is under close scrutiny to ascertain exactly how much to apply and when, especially in the crucial months of January and February.

Winemaker, Blair Walter, 'I want to produce the best possible Bannock-burn Pinot Noir.'

For the 2000 growing season, there was no irrigation at all, although there was plenty of water available naturally, and Walter is very happy with the results. Again it is a process of watching and learning as the weather patterns evolve and the vines age.

The key to the future at Felton Road has become Pinot Noir, and it is firmly in the forefront of planning and the approach of winemaker Walter.

'I want to produce the best possible Bannockburn Pinot Noir, and to do that I need to understand the top Pinots from Oregon, California and France, to find out how a particular winemaker made a great wine from their particular fruit,' he explains.

Much of this will happen in the vineyard, where the essential character of the wine is grown, not made. For this reason the company has decided that no fruit will be used from vineyards in which they do not have total control. This encompasses their own estate, plus other properties where they buy fruit but have full management control of the vines.

Naturally what the vineyard delivers seems to be great fruit clarity and no aggressive tannins or bitterness – points which are sharpened in the winery where there is no pumping or filtering of juice or wine. There is also the single-block philosophy which retains individual vineyard characteristics rather than blending them away into compound wines.

Yet vineyard control is far from the conclusive solution that it is often portrayed to be, as Walter concedes. 'Pinots coming off our vineyard can be very simple. The very cool ripening conditions can give us such pure fruit that the wines lack complexity,' he says.

The answer is to introduce complexity such as oak in the winery, yet the winemaking seems to be most concerned to keep its contribution to a minimum. Oak is carefully selected from the most delicate offerings, with Vosges a favoured source, and it is judiciously applied: in the case of Chardonnay with greater focus on older barrels. Pinot has as much as 30% new oak, all from Burgundian *tonneliers* with three-year-old dried staves

ABOVE: Pruning in the winter chill.

RIGHT: Frosty morning, Felton Road.

125

and minimal or no char. Spice to enhance the fruit is the intent.

All white wines are entirely wild-yeast fermented; pinot are partially, with the first three vats being started by inoculation, which then seems to trigger the rest. Over time it may be that all the wines will start fermentation spontaneously. Whole-bunch pressing, although only in part for Pinot Noir, is also a factor in this 'gently as possible' regime.

The style is to be unequivocally Felton Road. 'It is important for people to pick up a glass and say "That's Felton Road",' says Walter.

And they do. Not only has Felton Road become a New Zealand wine name of note and a hot international property, it has also become a financial success of the sort which attracts headlines. In 2000, Stuart Elms sold Felton Road to English businessman Nigel Greening, reportedly for millions of dollars more than most observers expected it to be worth. Greening is more than happy with his purchase, which he sees as a rising star with immense potential, and he intends to continue much as Elms and Walter began. With Walter still very much in charge of developing an inimitable Felton Road style, expect more of the same for the foreseeable future.

ABOVE: Riesling.
LEFT: 'We still don't really know how to grow the grapes well here, or how to make the best wine from them... We are learning.'